SIMPLY VEGAN

QUICK VEGETARIAN MEALS

BY DEBRA WASSERMAN

NUTRITION SECTION

BY REED MANGELS, PH.D., R.D.

BALTIMORE, MARYLAND

MARCH 1991

1994 –– FIFTH PRINTING

Reed Mangels completed her Ph.D. in Nutrition at the University of Maryland. She has worked as a dietitian in hospitals and in the community. Debra Wasserman earned an M.A. in International Relations from Georgetown University.

ACKNOWLEDGEMENTS

Special thanks to the following people who either edited or reviewed sections of this book: Charles Stahler, Arnold Alper, M.D., Karen Lazarus, M.S., M.D., Suzanne Havala, R.D., Jay Lavine, M.D., Jerome Marcus, M.D., Keith Akers, Terry Carlo, R.D., Kenneth Burke, Ph.D., R.D., Marion Nestle, Ph.D., M.P.H., Sally Clinton, Barbara Lovitts, and Carole Hamlin. Your encouragement and valuable comments added much to the final contents of this book. Thank you also to Janet Steinberg for doing the beautiful drawings found on the cover and throughout this book. And finally, thanks to friends who contributed recipes and to the many members of *The Vegetarian Resource Group* who tasted and commented on the recipes found in this book. These recipes were tested at potluck dinners, conferences, family gatherings, and other events over a two-year period.

DEFINITION OF VEGAN

Vegetarians do not eat meat, fish, and poultry. Vegans, in addition to being vegetarian, do not use other animal products and by-products including eggs, dairy products, honey, leather, fur, wool, soaps and toothpastes which contain lard, etc.

A vegan may abstain from eggs and dairy products for health, environmental, and/or ethical reasons. Though no direct killing results from eating eggs or dairy, a vegan feels that he or she is promoting the meat industry by consuming these products. Once the animals are too old to be productive, they are sold as meat. Since male calves do not produce milk, they usually are raised for veal or other products, and then killed. Male chickens may just be thrown away. Many people stay away from these products because of cruel factory farm conditions associated with their production.

The
VRg.
VEGETARIAN
Resource Group

FOREWORD

Simply Vegan is more than a cookbook. It is a guide to a non-violent, environmentally sound, humane life-style.

About ten years ago, I became vegan for ethical reasons. As a graduate student studying International Relations at Georgetown University, I often found myself having to justify my strong beliefs in pacifism. In course after course on foreign policy making, I felt that I was the only one in my graduate class who saw war as the last option for settling disputes. With the exception of one other classmate from Venezuela, I was the only student who truly believed in promoting non-violence.

One evening as I sat around the dinner table with several non-vegetarian classmates, one person asked me if I ate meat. I replied, "yes." To which he added, "Isn't killing animals for food a violent act?" My response was that animals are not people. However, after that evening's discussion I immediately became vegetarian. I quickly realized that killing animals for food was not only unnecessary and inconsistent with my own non-violent lifestyle, but that raising animals for food was destroying our environment and in many cases ruining our health, too.

As time goes on, I find that eating a vegan diet, using ecologically sound products that have not been tested on animals, and wearing clothes made from non-animal sources is not difficult, as long as you know where to shop for these items. Three years ago I saw the need to create a convenient guide to vegan living. *Simply Vegan* is that resource. I hope this book makes your life simpler.

-- Debra Wasserman
Baltimore, Maryland

Please Note: The contents of *Simply Vegan* are not intended to provide medical advice. Medical advice should be obtained from a qualified health professional.

TABLE OF CONTENTS

TIME-SAVING COOKING SUGGESTIONS

One purpose of *Simply Vegan* is to make vegan living as simple as possible. Most people follow a fast-paced lifestyle. Their hectic schedules leave them with little time to prepare elaborate vegan meals. Keeping this in mind we have included the following time-saving cooking tips, as well as information on using microwave ovens. Although Debra Wasserman, author of *Simply Vegan*, still doesn't own or use a microwave oven due to her concerns about its safeness, others, including Dr. Karen Lazarus, frequently use microwave ovens to prepare vegan meals.

HOW TO COOK VEGETABLES QUICKER

= = Slit green beans and carrots lengthwise
= = Shred cabbage and beets
= = Chop asparagus, broccoli, and cauliflower into flowerets
= = Cube squash and potatoes; boil them instead of baking them
= = Slice celery, bok choy, etc., on a 45 degree angle

OTHER TIME–SAVING IDEAS

= = Use basmati rice; it cooks quicker than brown rice
= = Use canned chickpeas (garbanzo beans), kidney beans, and other beans when in a rush; you may want to rinse out the salt from canned beans before cooking
= = When cooking brown rice or potatoes, make extras to be used for preparing another meal

MICROWAVE COOKING

The contributors to this book have different opinions about the use of microwave ovens. For example, Debra Wasserman does not use this appliance. On the other hand, Karen Lazarus finds microwave ovens to be a big time-saver, something she highly values while practicing medicine and raising a daughter.

Since the authors of this book recognize that many households own a microwave oven today, we decided to present a section on the considerations associated with using microwave ovens to prepare food. The following information was written by Karen Lazarus, M.D.

At first I resisted buying a microwave oven. Perhaps it was because I had heard so much about safety problems in early models, or perhaps it was because I had heard that foods did not taste or look the same when cooked in a microwave oven. I had also heard microwave ovens described as expensive potato bakers. But I learned that they were tremendous time-savers, and the demands of my family and professional commitments eventually led me to purchase some time-saving appliances, including a microwave oven. Within a short time I wondered why I had waited so long to obtain such a valuable piece of equipment.

Microwave ovens are quick, convenient, cool, and energy efficient appliances, that cook foods with a minimum of destruction to nutrients. As an example of its speed, one can bake a potato in six to ten minutes, depending on its size. The rapid cooking preserves heat sensitive nutrients, as it is prolonged exposure to high temperatures that results in destruction of vitamins. Microwave ovens are convenient because of their speed, and because you can reheat, or even cook some items in the same dishes you will use to eat the foods, thereby avoiding the need to clean extra pots. When defrosting frozen foods, if you have frozen them in microwavable containers, you can just place the food in the container in the microwave oven.

Microwave ovens stay cool. During the hot summer when you may be hesitant to light your gas or electric oven, the microwave oven will not heat up your kitchen. Even immediately after using it, both the outside and inside walls of the oven are safe to touch. However, although the dishes in which you cook will remain cooler than if placed in a conventional oven, they may become hot, especially with longer cooking, because of contact with the hot food. Even if you are able to remove a dish from the oven with your bare hands, you must remember to remove lids by opening the side away from you first to allow steam to escape on the other side, or you could burn yourself with the steam. Microwave ovens are energy efficient, using much less energy than a conventional oven, whether electric or gas.

Microwave ovens cannot completely replace other cooking methods. There will be no saving of time if you use a microwave oven to cook food that requires prolonged cooking for rehydration, such as pasta, rice, or dried beans, and you would need to use a very large bowl to prevent boiling over, so it is not worth using a microwave for these foods. Foods do not brown and become crisp in microwave ovens as they do in conventional ones, but on a vegan diet there are not as many foods that are browned as on an omnivorous diet, so this may not be a problem.

Of all the foods that I have cooked in a microwave oven, there are only two that I can think of that do not come out as well as they do when cooked in a conventional oven. One is the skin of a baked potato. If I were given a choice, I would prefer a potato baked in the conventional oven because of the texture of the skin. However, at home I eat more microwave baked potatoes because when I decide I want one, I usually do not want to wait over an hour to bake it, and I usually forget to put potatoes in my oven when I bake bread. I have never learned how to bake bread in a microwave oven, but it can be done. The second food that I prefer to bake in my conventional oven is a dessert made with fruit and matzoh which comes out crisp in my gas oven, and soft in the microwave oven. It probably tastes the same regardless of the cooking method, but the texture is different.

Microwave cooking is not as even as other methods. In order to rectify this, some ovens are built with a turntable that spins automatically when the oven cooks. My oven does not have a built-in turntable, but I purchased a separate one shortly after I purchased the oven. Although it does not spin as quickly as those that are built-in, I have never had much of a problem with uneven cooking, except for the food in the middle of a dish if I have not cooked it long enough.

Reed Mangels, Ph.D., R.D. adds that a recent article addresses another area of concern -- food containers and packaging used for microwaving. (Lefferts LY and Schmidt S: Microwaves: The heat is on. *Nutrition Action* 17: 1, 5-7, 1990) There is a possibility that potentially harmful substances could be released from "microwave-safe" containers, other plastic containers, and plastic wraps when these products are heated. If these containers or wraps are in contact with the food, the potentially harmful substances could migrate directly into the food. For now, I agree with Lefferts and Schmidts' recommendations: Only use glass or Corning Ware cookware in the microwave; Make sure food doesn't touch plastic wrap while cooking, or use glass covers or waxed paper; Avoid heat susceptor packaging (used to brown frozen microwaved french fries and crisp microwave popcorn).

SAMPLE MENUS

BREAKFASTS

I. Cindy's Light and Fluffy Pancakes (p. 23)
Peach Compote (p. 24)
Sauteed Potatoes (p. 25)
Orange Juice

II. Scrambled Tofu (p. 97)
Corn Bread (p. 21)
Baked Pears (p. 26)
Grape Juice

III. Oatmeal Plus (p. 23)
Sliced Bananas or Apples
Grape Juice or Soy milk

LUNCHES ON THE GO

I. Hummus (p. 27) on Pita Bread with Sprouts, Tomato, and Carrots
Pineapple Juice
Plums and Ginger Cookies (p. 109)

II. Fava Bean Spread (p. 28) on Whole Wheat Bread with Lettuce and sliced mushrooms
Apple Nut Salad (p. 41)
Popcorn (p. 34)
Orange Juice

III. Tofu Spread (p. 100) and whole wheat crackers
Cherry Tomatoes
Grape Juice
Apple

LUNCHES

I. Pasta Fruit Salad (p. 43)
    Corn Chowder (p. 45) and Pita Chips (p. 36)
    Thick Shake (p. 18)

II. Tempeh/Rice Pocket Sandwich (p. 94)
    Apple Juice and Green Salad (p. 39)
    Festive Cashew Cookies (p. 110)

III. Peanut Butter and Fruit on Whole Wheat Bread (p. 29)
    Carrot and Celery Sticks with plain soy yogurt dip
    Tomato Juice
    Creamy Rice Pudding (p. 115)

DINNERS

I. Carrot Salad
    Kale Cream Sauce over Pasta (p. 90)
    Breaded Okra (p. 64)
    Fruit Whiz (p. 17) and Melon

II. Easy Coleslaw (p. 40)
    Fava Bean Delight (p. 78) and Lemony Rice (p. 54)
    Water or Juice
    Pita Chips (p. 36)

III. Apple Nut Salad (p. 41)
    Hummus (p. 27) Sandwich on Whole Wheat Bread with
        sliced tomato and cucumber
    Corn Chowder (p. 45) and Grapes

IV. Stuffed Tomato Halves (p. 42)
    Barbecued Tempeh and Peaches (p. 95) with Plain Rice or
        Pasta
    Chocolate Pudding (p. 114)

V. Apple Celery Salad (p. 41)
    Tofu Chili (p. 107) and Steamed Squash (p. 55) with Rice
    Baked Papaya (p. 112)

MENU ANALYSIS

(Note: Menus are on the preceding two pages.)

Menu	RDA Male,25–50 Calories	63 Pro (gm)	Carb (gm)	Fat (gm)	Fat (%)	Vit A (IU)	60 Vit C (mg)
Breakfast 1	946	20	168	25	24	661	121
Breakfast 2	708	18	113	24	30	152	9
Breakfast 3	600	22	113	10	15	158	16
Go Lunch 1	688	16	126	17	22	8319	66
Go Lunch 2	665	22	114	18	24	401	123
Go Lunch 3	439	11	81	10	20	4022	27
Lunch 1	777	19	160	12	14	10650	84
Lunch 2	921	30	139	30	29	500	8
Lunch 3	622	23	102	18	27	21770	64
Dinner 1	902	22	152	27	27	26803	104
Dinner 2	741	25	133	15	18	6964	135
Dinner 3	786	22	131	27	31	9263	63
Dinner 4	747	29	127	18	7	3033	51
Dinner 5	733	27	142	10	12	5832	224

RDA Male,25–50	1.5 Thiamin (mg)	1.7 Ribo (mg)	19 Nia (mg)	800 Calcium (mg)	10 Iron (mg)
Breakfast 1	1	.4	7.4	271	4.7
Breakfast 2	.5	.4	3	331	10
Breakfast 3	1.9	.9	5.3	151	5.6
Go Lunch 1	.7	.45	5.2	295	5.6
Go Lunch 2	.6	.4	5.5	193	5.3
Go Lunch 3	.4	.4	2.6	190	6.4
Lunch 1	.7	.6	4.9	184	5.1
Lunch 2	2.3	.7	10.8	198	9.1
Lunch 3	.6	.4	8.1	184	6.2
Dinner 1	1.9	.9	8.1	248	6.7
Dinner 2	.7	.4	5.8	232	6.1
Dinner 3	.6	.4	5.1	315	6.6
Dinner 4	.6	.5	9.4	232	5.9
Dinner 5	.9	.4	7	292	10.1

TOP 15 RECIPES FOR CALCIUM

		mg Ca/serving	Page #
1.	Sesamiso Spread	481	30
2.	Pasta with Spicy Tahini Sauce	369	90
3.	Tofu Casserole	279	105
4.	Spicy Sauteed Tofu with Peas	261	103
5.	Mini Pizzas	235	34
6.	Bok Choy Stir-Fry	240	63
7.	Cindy's Light and Fluffy Pancakes	210	23
8.	Broccoli and Tofu Saute	194	103
9.	Scrambled Tofu and Bok Choy	190	96
10.	Hummus	178	27
11.	Wayne's Tofu Chili	164	107
12.	Cornbread	161	21
13.	Tofu Italiano	159	106
14.	Tofu Stew	153	104
15.	Tofu Squash Scramble	151	97

TOP 16 RECIPES FOR VITAMIN C

		mg Vitamin C/svg	Page #
1.	Tropical Fruit Smoothie	184	16
2.	Baked Papaya	118	112
3.	Blended Delight	112	18
4.	Wayne's Tofu Chili	90	107
5.	Cold Tomato Soup	86	48
6.	Red Hot Zucchini	77	56
7.	Fruit Whiz	75	17
8.	Sweet Orange Rice	73	53
9.	Broccoli Chow Mein	71	78
10.	Thick Shake	68	18
11.	Party Punch	67	19
12.	Mini Pizzas	67	34
13.	Fruit Fizz	55	19
14.	Broccoli and Tofu Saute	53	103
15.	Bok Choy and Carrots	53	63
16.	Bok Choy and Apple	53	64

TOP 16 RECIPES FOR IRON

		mg Iron/svg	Page #
1.	Spicy Sauteed Tofu with Peas	14	103
2.	Tofu Casserole	9	105
3.	Tofu Italiano	9	106
4.	Tofu Stew	8	104
5.	Wayne's Tofu Chili	8	107
6.	Broccoli and Tofu Saute	7	103
7.	Spicy Tofu Saute	7	101
8.	Scrambled Tofu and Bok Choy	7	96
9.	Tofu/Squash Scramble	7	97
10.	Tofu Squash Burgers	7	102
11.	Creamed Broccoli and Pasta	6	86
12.	Tofu Mushroom Sauce	6	101
13.	Tofu Dip	6	99
14.	Creamy Lentil Soup	6	49
15.	Sesamiso Spread	6	30
16.	Tofu "Coddies"	6	102

RECIPES

Recipe analysis was done with the Nutripak Professional Plus System (Nutrient Data Resources, Cleveland, Ohio) with additional information from manufacturers and food composition tables (1,2).

Optional ingredients were not included in calculations. For a range of servings such as 2-3, the lower number of servings was selected.

1. Lanza E and Butrum RR: A critical review of food fiber analysis and data. *Journal of the American Dietetic Association*, 86: 732-743, 1986.

2. Hurlbert I and Liebman B: Rough it up. *Nutrition Action*, 17: 8-9, 1990.

BEVERAGES

TROPICAL FRUIT SMOOTHIE

(Serves 2)

2 kiwi fruit, peeled
3 oranges, peeled and seeded
1 banana, peeled
6 ice cubes

Place all the ingredients in a blender and blend until smooth. Serve immediately.

Variations: Substitute different fruits such as pineapple, strawberries, or grapes.

TOTAL CALORIES PER SERVING: 192   % OF CALORIES FROM FAT: 4%
PROTEIN: 3 gm   CARBOHYDRATES: 48 gm   FAT: 1 gm
CALCIUM: 102 mg   IRON: .7 mg   SODIUM: 5 mg   DIETARY FIBER: 6 gm

FRUIT WHIZ

(Serves 2)

**1 Cup soy milk
1 teaspoon vanilla extract
2 large oranges, peeled and sectioned
1 large banana, peeled
5 ice cubes**

Place all the ingredients in a blender and blend until smooth. Serve immediately.

Variation: Substitute 3 peeled tangerines for the oranges. Make sure to remove all seeds before blending.

TOTAL CALORIES PER SERVING: 192   % OF CALORIES FROM FAT: 19%
PROTEIN: 7 gm   CARBOHYDRATES: 36 gm   FAT: 4 gm
CALCIUM: 98 mg   IRON: 1 mg   SODIUM: 66 mg   DIETARY FIBER: 4 gm

BLENDED DELIGHT

(Serves 4)

2 bananas, peeled
1 peach, peeled and pitted
6 strawberries
4 Cups orange juice

Place all the ingredients in a blender and blend until smooth. Chill and serve.

Variations: Substitute blueberries for strawberries and/or different fruit juices for orange juice.

TOTAL CALORIES PER SERVING: 178   % OF CALORIES FROM FAT: 2%
PROTEIN: 3 gm   CARBOHYDRATES: 44 gm   FAT: <1 gm
CALCIUM: 29 mg   IRON: 1 mg   SODIUM: 3 mg   DIETARY FIBER: 3 gm

THICK SHAKE

(Serves 3)

1 1/2 Cups soy milk
1 teaspoon vanilla extract
1 papaya, peeled and chopped
1 banana, peeled
1 Cup raisins

Place all the ingredients in a blender and blend until smooth. Serve immediately.

Variation: Substitute 2 peaches for the papaya.

TOTAL CALORIES PER SERVING: 317   % OF CALORIES FROM FAT: 12%
PROTEIN: 8 gm   CARBOHYDRATES: 69 gm   FAT: 4 gm
CALCIUM: 96 mg   IRON: 2 mg   SODIUM: 75 mg   DIETARY FIBER: 6 gm

PARTY PUNCH

(Serves 4)

1 pint cranberry juice
1 pint lemonade
Liter bottle of ginger ale or club soda
1 orange, sliced
Ice

Mix all the ingredients in a large punch bowl and serve.

Variations: Use different juices and/or replace orange slices with lemon slices.

TOTAL CALORIES PER SERVING: 222   % OF CALORIES FROM FAT: 1%
PROTEIN: <1 gm   CARBOHYDRATES: 57 gm   FAT: <1 gm
CALCIUM: 28 mg   IRON: 1 mg   SODIUM: 23 mg   DIETARY FIBER: <1 gm

FRUIT FIZZ

(Serves 2)

5 ounces crushed pineapple
1 Cup orange juice
1 apple, peeled, diced, and cored
1 pear, peeled, diced, and cored
14 ounces club soda

Place all the ingredients in a blender and blend until smooth. Chill and serve.

TOTAL CALORIES PER SERVING: 163   % OF CALORIES FROM FAT: 3%
PROTEIN: 1 gm   CARBOHYDRATES: 41 gm   FAT: <1 gm
CALCIUM: 33 mg   IRON: <1 mg   SODIUM: 48 mg   DIETARY FIBER: 4 gm

BREAKFASTS

APPLE RAISIN SPICE MUFFINS

(Makes 18)

1 Cup unbleached white flour
2 Cups whole wheat pastry flour
1 teaspoon baking powder
1/2 teaspoon baking soda
1 teaspoon cinnamon
1/4 teaspoon nutmeg
1/2 teaspoon allspice
1 Cup water
1/3 Cup maple syrup or molasses
2 apples, cored and chopped finely
1/2 Cup raisins

Preheat oven to 400 degrees. Mix all the ingredients together in a large bowl. Pour batter into lightly oiled muffin tins. Bake for 20 minutes at 400 degrees.

Cool muffins before removing from tins.

Variation: Add 1/2 cup chopped walnuts to batter before baking.

TOTAL CALORIES EACH: 106   % OF CALORIES FROM FAT: 3%
PROTEIN: 3 gm   CARBOHYDRATES: 24 gm   FAT: <1 gm
CALCIUM: 20 mg   IRON: <1 mg   SODIUM: 32 mg   DIETARY FIBER: 2 gm

BANANA MUFFINS

(Makes 18)

4–5 bananas (approximately 2 Cups)
1 Cup raisins (If hard, soften by soaking in apple juice.)
3 Cups rolled oats
1 Tablespoon cinnamon
1 Tablespoon baking powder
1/2 Cup almond or peanut butter

Preheat oven to 350 degrees. Mash bananas. Add the remaining ingredients and mix well. Pour batter into lightly oiled muffin tins. Bake 25 minutes at 350 degrees.

Cool muffins before removing from tins.

Variation: Substitute 1/3 cup oil for nut butter.

TOTAL CALORIES EACH: 154   % OF CALORIES FROM FAT: 31%
PROTEIN: 4 gm   CARBOHYDRATES: 25 gm   FAT: 5 gm
CALCIUM: 61 mg   IRON: 1 mg   SODIUM: 3 mg   DIETARY FIBER: 3 gm

CORN BREAD

(Serves 6)

1 Cup cornmeal
1 Cup whole wheat flour
1 Tablespoon baking powder
1/4 Cup oil
1 Cup soy milk
1/3 Cup molasses or maple syrup

Preheat oven to 375 degrees. Mix ingredients together in a bowl. Pour batter into lightly oiled 8-inch round pan. Bake for 20 minutes.

Variation: Prepare same batter; however, pour batter into lightly oiled muffin tins and bake at the same temperature for the same amount of time. Children will especially enjoy these muffins.

TOTAL CALORIES PER SERVING: 299   % OF CALORIES FROM FAT: 33%
PROTEIN: 6 gm   CARBOHYDRATES: 46 gm   FAT: 11 gm
CALCIUM: 161 mg   IRON: 3 mg   SODIUM: 29 mg   DIETARY FIBER: 2 gm

OATMEAL MEDLEY

(Serves 3)

2 Cups rolled oats
4 Cups water
1/2 Cup unsweetened shredded coconut
1/2 teaspoon cinnamon
1 Cup fresh or frozen blueberries

Mix ingredients (except for blueberries) together in a pot. Cook over medium heat for about 10 minutes until oats are done. Stir oats occasionally while cooking.

Add blueberries and heat for 3 more minutes. Serve hot.

Variation: Substitute strawberries or other chopped fruit for blueberries.

TOTAL CALORIES PER SERVING: 325   % OF CALORIES FROM FAT: 34%
PROTEIN: 10 gm   CARBOHYDRATES: 45 gm   FAT: 12 gm
CALCIUM: 37 mg   IRON: 3 mg   SODIUM: 8 mg   DIETARY FIBER: 5 gm

OATMEAL PLUS

(Serves 2)

1/2 Cup rolled oats
1 Cup water
1/8 Cup nutritional yeast
1/4 Cup wheat germ
1 Cup soy milk

Place oats and water in large microwaveable bowl (at least 1 quart size). Microwave on high for 4 minutes and 10 seconds (or cook in pot on stove until thickened). Add nutritional yeast, wheat germ, and soy milk. Mix together.

Variation: Add raisins or other dried fruit.

TOTAL CALORIES PER SERVING: 211   % OF CALORIES FROM FAT: 26%
PROTEIN: 14 gm   CARBOHYDRATES: 28 gm   FAT: 6 gm
CALCIUM: 76 mg   IRON: 4 mg   SODIUM: 76 mg   DIETARY FIBER: 3 gm

CINDY'S LIGHT AND FLUFFY PANCAKES

(Serves 4)

2 Cups whole wheat pastry flour
1/2 Cup cornmeal
2 Tablespoons Ener-G Egg Replacer or cornstarch
2 teaspoons baking powder
1/2 teaspoon baking soda
1/2 teaspoon cinnamon
1/4 Cup oil
1 3/4 to 2 Cups soy milk
1/8 Cup maple syrup
1/4 teaspoon apple cider vinegar

Mix dry ingredients together. Then add the remaining ingredients.

Make sure all the ingredients are mixed together well. Batter should be spongy -- not runny or thick. Preheat lightly oiled frying pan over medium heat. Pour a ladle full of batter into pan and cook on both sides until golden brown. Makes 5 large pancakes.

TOTAL CALORIES PER SERVING: 493   % OF CALORIES FROM FAT: 33%
PROTEIN: 14 gm   CARBOHYDRATES: 73 gm   FAT: 18 gm
CALCIUM: 210 mg   IRON: 3 mg   SODIUM: 201 mg   DIETARY FIBER: 5 gm

(Note: Ener-G Egg Replacer can be purchased at some natural foods stores or through the mail. See page 209.)

PEACH COMPOTE

(Serves 3)

3 peaches, pitted and chopped
1/3 Cup raisins
2 Tablespoons apple juice concentrate
2 Tablespoons water

Heat all the ingredients together over medium-high heat for 3 minutes. Lower heat and simmer for 20 minutes longer. Serve hot over pancakes or French toast.

TOTAL CALORIES PER SERVING: 111   % OF CALORIES FROM FAT: 2%
PROTEIN: 1 gm   CARBOHYDRATES: 29 gm   FAT: <1 gm
CALCIUM: 16 mg   IRON: <1 mg   SODIUM: 3 mg   DIETARY FIBER: 3 gm

FRUIT FRENCH TOAST

(Serves 2)

1 banana, peeled
4 large strawberries, fresh or frozen
1/3 Cup apple juice
1/2 teaspoon cinnamon
4 slices whole wheat bread

Blend together first four ingredients. Soak bread in the fruit mixture. Cook on both sides on lightly oiled or non-stick griddle until just beginning to brown.

Variation: Use other fruits such as pineapple or blueberries.

TOTAL CALORIES PER SERVING: 191   % OF CALORIES FROM FAT: 8%
PROTEIN: 6 gm   CARBOHYDRATES: 42 gm   FAT: 2 gm
CALCIUM: 55 mg   IRON: 2 mg   SODIUM: 243 mg   DIETARY FIBER: 5 gm

SAUTEED POTATOES

(Serves 4)

6 potatoes, cleaned and thinly sliced
2 Tablespoons oil
1 onion, finely chopped
1/2 teaspoon garlic powder
1/4 teaspoon paprika
Pepper and salt to taste

Stir-fry ingredients together in a large frying pan for 20 to 25 minutes over medium-high heat until potatoes are tender. Stir often so potatoes do not stick to pan. Serve hot.

TOTAL CALORIES PER SERVING: 243   % OF CALORIES FROM FAT: 26%
PROTEIN: 4 gm   CARBOHYDRATES: 42 gm   FAT: 7 gm
CALCIUM: 22 mg   IRON: <1 mg   SODIUM: 11 mg   DIETARY FIBER: 4 gm

FRIED BANANAS

(Serves 2)

3 very ripe bananas, peeled
1 Tablespoon oil
1/4 teaspoon cinnamon

Heat oil in a frying pan over medium heat. Slice bananas in half lengthwise.
Lay bananas in pan. Sprinkle with cinnamon. Fry on each side for 2 minutes.
Serve hot.

TOTAL CALORIES PER SERVING: 218   % OF CALORIES FROM FAT: 31%
PROTEIN: 2 gm   CARBOHYDRATES: 40 gm   FAT: 8 gm
CALCIUM: 10 mg   IRON: <1 mg   SODIUM: 2 mg   DIETARY FIBER: 2 gm

BAKED PEARS

(Serves 2)

2 large pears, cored and sliced
1 teaspoon cinnamon
1/4 Cup water

Preheat oven to 425 degrees. Lay pears in a baking pan. Sprinkle with
cinnamon and water. Bake for 25 minutes at 425 degrees. Serve hot.

Variation: Add raisins before baking.

TOTAL CALORIES PER SERVING: 98   % OF CALORIES FROM FAT: 6%
PROTEIN: <1 gm   CARBOHYDRATES: 25 gm   FAT: <1 gm
CALCIUM: 18 mg   IRON: <1 mg   SODIUM: 0 mg   DIETARY FIBER: 6 gm

SANDWICHES

CHICKPEA ITALIANA

(Makes 6 sandwiches)

19-ounce can chickpeas or garbanzo beans, drained and
    mashed
1/4 teaspoon oregano
1/8 teaspoon pepper
1/4 teaspoon onion powder
4 Tablespoons tomato sauce

Mix all the ingredients together in a bowl. Serve on whole wheat bread
with lettuce.

TOTAL CALORIES PER SERVING: 98   % OF CALORIES FROM FAT: 8%
PROTEIN: 4 gm   CARBOHYDRATES: 19 gm   FAT: 1 gm
CALCIUM: 27 mg   IRON: 1 mg   SODIUM: 301 mg   DIETARY FIBER: 3 gm

HUMMUS

(Makes 6 sandwiches)

1 large onion, chopped
2 cloves garlic, minced
2 Tablespoons oil (olive oil is best)
19-ounce can chickpeas or garbanzo beans, drained
1/2 Cup tahini (sesame butter)
1/4 Cup lemon juice or juice from 1 fresh lemon
1/4 teaspoon pepper
1/8 teaspoon cayenne pepper
1/3 Cup chopped parsley (optional)
3 Tablespoons water

Saute onions and garlic in oil until onions are transparent. Pour into a blender or food processor. Add remaining ingredients. Blend until mixture is smooth, adding a little more water if necessary. Serve on whole wheat bread or in pita bread with chopped lettuce or sprouts and tomato, or as a dip with raw vegetables and crackers.

TOTAL CALORIES PER SERVING: 222   % OF CALORIES FROM FAT: 47%
PROTEIN: 7 gm   CARBOHYDRATES: 26 gm   FAT: 12 gm
CALCIUM: 178 mg   IRON: 2 mg   SODIUM: 280 mg   DIETARY FIBER: 5 gm

GARBANZO SPREAD

(Makes 6 sandwiches)

19-ounce can chickpeas or garbanzo beans, drained
1/2 Cup tomato sauce
1-2 teaspoons cumin
1-2 teaspoons garlic powder

Blend all the ingredients together in a blender or food processor. Serve on whole wheat bread with lettuce.

TOTAL CALORIES PER SERVING: 102   % OF CALORIES FROM FAT: 8%
PROTEIN: 4 gm   CARBOHYDRATES: 20 gm   FAT: 1 gm
CALCIUM: 28 mg   IRON: 1 mg   SODIUM: 363 mg   DIETARY FIBER: 1 gm

FAVA BEAN SPREAD

(Makes 6 sandwiches)

19-ounce can fava beans, drained
1/4 Cup tahini (sesame butter)
1 Tablespoon lemon juice
1 teaspoon garlic powder

1 Tablespoon olive oil
1/4 Cup water

Blend all the ingredients together in a blender or food processor until smooth. Serve on whole wheat bread with lettuce.

TOTAL CALORIES PER SERVING: 120   % OF CALORIES FROM FAT: 41%
PROTEIN: 6 gm   CARBOHYDRATES: 14 gm   FAT: 6 gm
CALCIUM: 95 mg   IRON: 2 mg   SODIUM: 406 mg   DIETARY FIBER: 4 gm

PEANUT BUTTER AND FRUIT

(1 sandwich)

1 Tablespoon peanut butter
1/2 fresh fruit (apple, pear, banana, peach, etc.), thinly sliced

Spread peanut butter on your favorite bread. Place slices of fresh fruit on the peanut butter. Enjoy!

Variation: Substitute dried fruit (apricots, figs, apples, pears, raisins, etc.) for the fresh fruit.

TOTAL CALORIES PER SERVING: 136   % OF CALORIES FROM FAT: 56%
PROTEIN: 5 gm   CARBOHYDRATES: 13 gm   FAT: 9 gm
CALCIUM: 10 mg   IRON: <1 mg   SODIUM: 76 mg   DIETARY FIBER: 3 gm

HOT BEAN SPREAD

(Makes 2-3 sandwiches)

1 Cup homemade or canned vegetarian baked beans
1 Tablespoon horseradish or more if desired
1/2 small onion, minced

Mash the beans in a bowl. Add the horseradish and onion. Mix well. Spread on two slices of whole wheat bread. Serve with lettuce and tomato slices.

TOTAL CALORIES PER SERVING: 112   % OF CALORIES FROM FAT: 9%
PROTEIN: 6 gm   CARBOHYDRATES: 25 gm   FAT: 1 gm
CALCIUM: 51 mg   IRON: 1 mg   SODIUM: 423 mg   DIETARY FIBER: 9 gm

SWEET BEAN SPREAD

(Makes 2-3 sandwiches)

1 Cup homemade or canned vegetarian baked beans
2 Tablespoons sweet pickle relish

Mash the beans in a bowl. Add the relish and mix well. Spread on whole wheat bread and add a few lettuce leaves.

TOTAL CALORIES PER SERVING: 120   % OF CALORIES FROM FAT: 8%
PROTEIN: 5 gm   CARBOHYDRATES: 27 gm   FAT: 1 gm
CALCIUM: 43 mg   IRON: 1 mg   SODIUM: 518 mg   DIETARY FIBER: 9 gm

SESAMISO SPREAD

(Makes 2 Sandwiches)

1/2 Cup tahini (sesame butter)
1/2 Cup red or brown (preferred) miso

Mix the tahini and miso together to form a paste. Spread in pita bread or on whole wheat bread. Add some lettuce, sliced tomatoes, sprouts, and chopped scallions. You may also want to add a slice of green pepper.

TOTAL CALORIES PER SERVING: 372   % OF CALORIES FROM FAT: 54%
PROTEIN: 15 gm   CARBOHYDRATES: 35 gm   FAT: 22 gm
CALCIUM: 481 mg   IRON: 6 mg   SODIUM: 2620 mg   DIETARY FIBER: 6 gm

OAT NUT BURGERS

(Makes 6)

2/3 Cup rolled oats
2/3 Cup chopped walnuts
1 large onion, chopped
3 stalks celery, chopped
2 carrots, grated
1/4 Cup whole wheat pastry or unbleached white flour
1/4 Cup water

Mix the ingredients together and season to taste. Shape into 6 burgers and fry 10 minutes on each side until brown.

TOTAL CALORIES PER SERVING: 156   % OF CALORIES FROM FAT: 50%
PROTEIN: 6 gm   CARBOHYDRATES: 16 gm   FAT: 9 gm
CALCIUM: 33 mg   IRON: 1 mg   SODIUM: 27 mg   DIETARY FIBER: 3 gm

GARBANZO BEAN BURGERS

(Makes 6)

2 Cups garbanzo beans (chickpeas), mashed
1 stalk celery, finely chopped
1 carrot, finely chopped
1/4 small onion, minced
1/4 Cup whole wheat flour
Salt and pepper to taste
2 teaspoons oil

Mix the ingredients (except oil) in a bowl. Form 6 flat patties. Fry in oiled pan over medium-high heat until burgers are golden brown on each side.

TOTAL CALORIES PER SERVING: 133   % OF CALORIES FROM FAT: 17%
PROTEIN: 5 gm   CARBOHYDRATES: 23 gm   FAT: 3 gm
CALCIUM: 34 mg   IRON: 1 mg   SODIUM: 250 mg   DIETARY FIBER: 2 gm

SNACKS

GARLIC BEAN DIP

(Serves 2)

1/3 pound green beans
2 cloves garlic, minced
1/2 teaspoon onion powder
1 1/2 Tablespoons tahini (sesame butter)
1 teaspoon soy sauce or tamari

Steam green beans for 10 minutes in about a cup of water until tender, yet firm. Rinse beans under cold water when done.

Meanwhile, place remaining ingredients in a blender or food processor. Add cooked beans. Blend 2 minutes or until creamy. Serve with crackers.

TOTAL CALORIES PER SERVING: 69   % OF CALORIES FROM FAT: 47%
PROTEIN: 3 gm   CARBOHYDRATES: 9 gm   FAT: 4 gm
CALCIUM: 121 mg   IRON: 1 mg   SODIUM: 203 mg   DIETARY FIBER: 3 gm

SPICY NACHO "CHEESE" DIP

(Serves 8)

1 1/2 Cups nutritional yeast
2/3 Cup whole wheat pastry or unbleached white flour
2 1/3 Cups water
1/2 Cup soy margarine
1 teaspoon garlic powder
1 Tablespoon mustard
1/3 Cup hot cherry peppers, diced

Mix yeast, flour, and water together in a pot. Cook over medium heat, stirring occasionally, until mixture boils. Add margarine. Allow to boil for one minute, then remove from heat.

Add garlic powder, mustard, and hot cherry peppers. Mix well.

Serve hot or chilled with crackers, chips or raw vegetables.

TOTAL CALORIES PER SERVING: 210   % OF CALORIES FROM FAT: 50%
PROTEIN: 11 gm   CARBOHYDRATES: 18 gm   FAT: 12 gm
CALCIUM: 64 mg   IRON: 5 mg   SODIUM: 186 mg   DIETARY FIBER: <1 gm

QUICK SALSA

(Serves 8)

29-ounce can tomato puree
2 ripe tomatoes, chopped
1 green pepper, chopped
4 scallions, chopped
1/4 teaspoon cayenne pepper
1 teaspoon garlic powder
Salt to taste (optional)

Mix all the ingredients together in a large bowl. Serve with chips.

Variation: Add more cayenne pepper to make salsa hotter!

TOTAL CALORIES PER SERVING: 44   % OF CALORIES FROM FAT: 6%
PROTEIN: 2 gm   CARBOHYDRATES: 10 gm   FAT: <1 gm
CALCIUM: 25 mg   IRON: 1 mg   SODIUM: 670 mg   DIETARY FIBER: 2 gm

POPCORN TREAT

(As many servings as you would like)

Popcorn
nutritional yeast

Pop popcorn in an air popper until done. Sprinkle with nutritional yeast.

TOTAL CALORIES PER 3 CUP SERVING: 138   % OF CALORIES FROM FAT: 12%
PROTEIN: 5 gm   CARBOHYDRATES: 28 gm   FAT: 2 gm
CALCIUM: 4 mg   IRON: 1 mg   SODIUM: 0 mg   DIETARY FIBER: 3 gm

MINI PIZZAS

(Serves 2-3)

**1 stalk broccoli, chopped
2 stalks celery, chopped finely
1 onion, minced
1/2 teaspoon oregano
1/2 teaspoon garlic powder
2 Tablespoons oil
15-ounce can tomato sauce
3 English muffins containing no animal products**

Saute broccoli, celery, onion, oregano, and garlic powder in oil over medium-high heat for 5 minutes, until broccoli is tender, yet firm.

Add tomato sauce and continue heating for 3 minutes longer. Remove from heat.

Split English muffins in half. Spoon sauce over muffins. Sprinkle with nutritional yeast if desired.

Bake at 400 degrees for 12 minutes. Serve pizza hot.

Variation: Substitute different vegetables in sauce such as mushrooms, green pepper, cauliflower, etc.

TOTAL CALORIES PER SERVING: 434   % OF CALORIES FROM FAT: 33%
PROTEIN: 13 gm   CARBOHYDRATES: 65 gm   FAT: 16 gm
CALCIUM: 235 mg   IRON: 5 mg   SODIUM: 2004 mg   DIETARY FIBER: 6 gm

COCONUT CHAPPATIS

(Serves 2)

1/2 Cup whole wheat pastry or unbleached white flour
1/3 Cup shredded coconut
1/2 teaspoon cinnamon
4 Tablespoons water

Mix ingredients together to form a firm dough. Divide into 4 equal parts. On floured board, roll each piece into a 1/4-inch thick circle.

Cook chappatis in an oiled pan over medium heat until light brown on each side. Serve warm.

TOTAL CALORIES PER SERVING: 181   % OF CALORIES FROM FAT: 44%
PROTEIN: 5 gm   CARBOHYDRATES: 23 gm   FAT: 9 gm
CALCIUM: 19 mg   IRON: 2 mg   SODIUM: 4 mg   DIETARY FIBER: unknown

PEANUT BUTTER COCONUT BALLS

(Serves 3)

1 ripe banana, mashed
1/2 pound peanut butter
1 ounce shredded coconut

Add mashed banana to peanut butter and mix well. Form 1-inch round balls.
Roll in coconut. Refrigerate until serving.

TOTAL CALORIES PER SERVING: 539   % OF CALORIES FROM FAT: 74%
PROTEIN: 23 gm   CARBOHYDRATES: 22 gm   FAT: 44 gm
CALCIUM: 31 mg   IRON: 2 mg   SODIUM: 365 mg   DIETARY FIBER: 6 gm

PITA CHIPS

(Serves 8)

**3 pita breads
2 teaspoons oil
1 teaspoon paprika
1 teaspoon garlic powder
1 teaspoon oregano
1/2 teaspoon salt (optional)**

Split pita breads in half. Cut each half into several 2-inch size triangles.

Place the cut bread on a lightly oiled cookie sheet. Sprinkle bread with half
the oil, and half the paprika, garlic powder, oregano, and if you prefer, salt.

Place the bread under a broiler until it begins to brown. Turn the bread over
and sprinkle with remaining oil and spices. Place the bread back under the
broiler for 2 minutes longer. Remove the chips. Once the chips cool they will
be crisp and delicious.

TOTAL CALORIES PER SERVING: 49   % OF CALORIES FROM FAT: 26%
PROTEIN: 2 gm   CARBOHYDRATES: 8 gm   FAT: 1 gm
CALCIUM: 12 mg   IRON: <1 mg   SODIUM: 81 mg   DIETARY FIBER: <1 gm

CHEESY PITA TOAST

(Serves 2)

2 pita breads
2 Tablespoons nutritional yeast
2 Tablespoons soy margarine

Split pita breads in half. Sprinkle nutritional yeast over bread and dab with margarine. Heat in a toaster oven for a few minutes, until margarine melts. Serve warm.

TOTAL CALORIES PER SERVING: 227   % OF CALORIES FROM FAT: 47%
PROTEIN: 7 gm   CARBOHYDRATES: 24 gm   FAT: 12 gm
CALCIUM: 52 mg   IRON: 2 mg   SODIUM: 354 mg   DIETARY FIBER: <1 gm

Please Note: If you are on a low-fat diet, we suggest eating fresh fruit or raw vegetables as a snack whenever possible.

SALADS

HEARTY GREEN LEAF SALAD

(Serves 4)

6 leaves green leaf lettuce, washed
1 stalk celery, chopped
1 apple, cored and chopped
1/2 Cup walnuts, chopped or whole

Tear lettuce leaves into bite-size pieces and place them in a large salad bowl. Add chopped celery, apples and walnuts. Top with your favorite dressing or use the following one.

TOTAL CALORIES PER SERVING: 121   % OF CALORIES FROM FAT: 67%
PROTEIN: 4 gm   CARBOHYDRATES: 8 gm   FAT: 9 gm
CALCIUM: 21 mg   IRON: 1 mg   SODIUM: 12 mg   DIETARY FIBER: 2 gm

FRUITY SALAD DRESSING

(Serves 4)

1 apple, cored and chopped
1/3 Cup water
1/4 Cup orange juice
1/8 teaspoon cinnamon

Place all the ingredients in a blender and blend at high speed for 2 minutes. Serve over your hearty green leaf salad.

TOTAL CALORIES PER SERVING: 27   % OF CALORIES FROM FAT: 3%
PROTEIN: <1 gm   CARBOHYDRATES: 7 gm   FAT: <1 gm
CALCIUM: 4 mg   IRON: <1 mg   SODIUM: <1 mg   DIETARY FIBER: <1 gm

GREEN SALAD AND TANGERINE DRESSING

(Serves 4)

6 leaves green leaf lettuce
2 tangerines, peeled and sectioned
1/3 Cup orange juice

Wash lettuce leaves and tear into bite-size pieces. Place lettuce in a large salad bowl.

Remove seeds from tangerine sections. Chop half the tangerine sections and place in salad bowl with lettuce. Place the remaining tangerine sections in a blender. Add the orange juice and blend at high speed for 1 minute. Pour tangerine dressing over lettuce and tangerine sections. Toss well. Top salad with the following spicy croutons.

TOTAL CALORIES PER SERVING: 32   % OF CALORIES FROM FAT: 3%
PROTEIN: 1 gm   CARBOHYDRATES: 8 gm   FAT: <1 gm
CALCIUM: 13 mg   IRON: <1 mg   SODIUM: 4 mg   DIETARY FIBER: 1 gm

SPICY SALAD CROUTONS

(Serves 4)

3 slices of whole wheat bread, cubed
1 Tablespoon olive oil
1/2 teaspoon garlic powder
1/8 teaspoon cayenne pepper
1/2 teaspoon basil

Mix all the ingredients together in a bowl. Spread the mixture on a baking pan. Broil for 3 minutes, stirring once, and remove from oven. Let the croutons cool for a few minutes. Serve over green salad with dressing.

TOTAL CALORIES PER SERVING: 72   % OF CALORIES FROM FAT: 49%
PROTEIN: 2 gm   CARBOHYDRATES: 8 gm   FAT: 4 gm
CALCIUM: 17 mg   IRON: 1 mg   SODIUM: 91 mg   DIETARY FIBER: 1 gm

COLESLAW

(Serves 8)

Small head green cabbage or 1/2 head small green cabbage plus 1/2 head small red cabbage, shredded
1 small container plain soy yogurt
1 Tablespoon lemon juice
1 teaspoon mustard
Pepper and salt to taste

Mix all the ingredients together in a bowl. If time permits, chill for 1 hour before serving. Toss well and serve.

TOTAL CALORIES PER SERVING: 25   % OF CALORIES FROM FAT: 25%
PROTEIN: 2 gm   CARBOHYDRATES: 3 gm   FAT: 1 gm
CALCIUM: 35 mg   IRON: <1 mg   SODIUM: 31 mg   DIETARY FIBER: 2 gm

EASY COLESLAW

(Serves 8-10)

Medium head green cabbage
2 large carrots
1/2 Cup eggless mayonnaise
1/4 Cup lemon juice
1/2 teaspoon celery seed
Dash of pepper
Salt to taste (optional)

Grate cabbage and carrots. Pour into a large bowl. Add the remaining ingredients and toss well. If time permits serve chilled.

TOTAL CALORIES PER SERVING: 68   % OF CALORIES FROM FAT: 56%
PROTEIN: 2 gm   CARBOHYDRATES: 8 gm   FAT: 4 gm
CALCIUM: 40 mg   IRON: 1 mg   SODIUM: 67 mg   DIETARY FIBER: 3 gm

APPLE CELERY SALAD

(Serves 4)

3 apples, cored and chopped finely
1 stalk celery, chopped finely
1 teaspoon cinnamon
1/2 Cup apple juice

Mix all the ingredients together in a bowl. If time permits, serve chilled.

TOTAL CALORIES PER SERVING: 77   % OF CALORIES FROM FAT: 5%
PROTEIN: <1 gm   CARBOHYDRATES: 20 gm   FAT: <1 gm
CALCIUM: 13 mg   IRON: <1 mg   SODIUM: 10 mg   DIETARY FIBER: 3 gm

APPLE NUT SALAD

(Serves 4)

3 apples, cored and chopped finely
1/2 Cup walnuts, chopped
1 teaspoon cinnamon
2/3 Cup orange juice

Mix all the ingredients together in a bowl. If time permits, serve chilled.

TOTAL CALORIES PER SERVING: 174   % OF CALORIES FROM FAT: 48%
PROTEIN: 4 gm   CARBOHYDRATES: 22 gm   FAT: 9 gm
CALCIUM: 20 mg   IRON: 1 mg   SODIUM: <1 mg   DIETARY FIBER: 4 gm

CABBAGE SALAD

(Serves 6)

1/2 head small green cabbage, shredded
2 carrots, grated
1 celery stalk, chopped finely or 1/2 teaspoon celery seed
1 clove garlic, minced or 1/2 teaspoon garlic powder
Pinch of pepper
1/4 Cup oil
1/4 Cup vinegar
1/2 Cup water

Mix all the ingredients together in a bowl. If time permits, serve chilled.

TOTAL CALORIES PER SERVING: 105   % OF CALORIES FROM FAT: 79%
PROTEIN: 1 gm   CARBOHYDRATES: 6 gm   FAT: 9 gm
CALCIUM: 32 mg   IRON: <1 mg   SODIUM: 23 mg   DIETARY FIBER: 2 gm

STUFFED TOMATO HALVES

(Serves 4)

4 tomatoes
1 small zucchini, grated
1/4 Cup orange juice
1/2 teaspoon garlic powder
1/4 teaspoon oregano
Pepper and salt to taste

Cut a hole in top of each tomato and carefully remove pulp. Place pulp into a bowl and add grated zucchini and other ingredients. Mix well and stuff mixture into tomatoes. If time permits, serve chilled.

TOTAL CALORIES PER SERVING: 41   % OF CALORIES FROM FAT: 9%
PROTEIN: 2 gm   CARBOHYDRATES: 10 gm   FAT: <1 gm
CALCIUM: 21 mg   IRON: 1 mg   SODIUM: 12 mg   DIETARY FIBER: 2 gm

AVOCADO BOATS

(Serves 4)

2 ripe avocados
1/2 ripe tomato, finely chopped
1/3 cucumber, finely chopped
1/4 teaspoon garlic powder
1 teaspoon lemon juice
Pinch cayenne pepper
Salt to taste

Carefully cut avocados in half lengthwise and remove seed. Remove avocado pulp from shell and mash in a bowl. Add other ingredients and mix well. Put mixture back into avocado shells. Serve alone or with chips or raw carrot and celery sticks.

TOTAL CALORIES PER SERVING: 167   % OF CALORIES FROM FAT: 84%
PROTEIN: 2 gm   CARBOHYDRATES: 9 gm   FAT: 16 gm
CALCIUM: 15 mg   IRON: 1 mg   SODIUM: 12 mg   DIETARY FIBER: unknown

PASTA FRUIT SALAD

(Serves 4)

2 Cups cooked pasta
2 apples, cored and chopped
2 scallions, finely chopped
5-ounce can water chestnuts, drained and chopped
1 teaspoon tarragon
1/2 Cup raisins

Mix all the ingredients together in a bowl. If time permits, chill before serving.

TOTAL CALORIES PER SERVING: 221   % OF CALORIES FROM FAT: 3%
PROTEIN: 4 gm   CARBOHYDRATES: 52 gm   FAT: 1 gm
CALCIUM: 31 mg   IRON: 1 mg   SODIUM: 7 mg   DIETARY FIBER: 4 gm

EASY PASTA SALAD

(Serves 8)

1 pound pasta, cooked and drained
8–ounce pkg. frozen lima beans, cooked
3 carrots, peeled and finely chopped
1 teaspoon dill weed
1/2 teaspoon salt (optional)
4 Tablespoons eggless mayonnaise

Mix all the ingredients together in a bowl. If time permits, chill before serving.

TOTAL CALORIES PER SERVING: 217   % OF CALORIES FROM FAT: 11%
PROTEIN: 8 gm   CARBOHYDRATES: 41 gm   FAT: 3 gm
CALCIUM: 27 mg   IRON: 2 mg   SODIUM: 41 mg   DIETARY FIBER: 3 gm

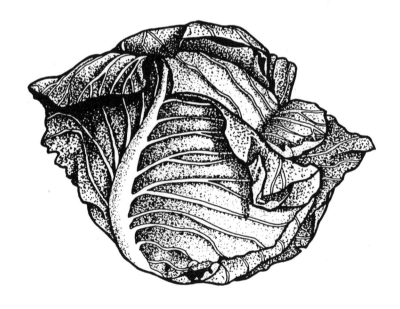

SOUPS

CORN CHOWDER

(Serves 5)

1 Tablespoon oil
1 onion, chopped
2 Cups water
2 stalks celery, chopped
2 carrots, chopped
two 17-ounce cans vegan creamed corn
1 Cup soy milk
1 potato, chopped
1 1/2 teaspoons garlic powder
1/4 teaspoon nutmeg
Salt and pepper to taste

Saute onion in oil over medium-high heat until soft. Add water and chopped celery and carrots. Cook 10 minutes. Add creamed corn, soy milk, chopped potato, and spices. Continue cooking for another 10 minutes. Serve hot.

TOTAL CALORIES PER SERVING: 166   % OF CALORIES FROM FAT: 25%
PROTEIN: 5 gm   CARBOHYDRATES: 30 gm   FAT: 5 gm
CALCIUM: 40 mg   IRON: 1 mg   SODIUM: 315 mg   DIETARY FIBER: 4 gm

QUICK CABBAGE SOUP

(Serves 2)

2 Cups Chinese cabbage or green cabbage, shredded
2 teaspoons oil
3 Cups water
1 vegetable bouillon cube

Saute cabbage in oil for 2 minutes over medium-high heat. Add water and bouillon cube. Continue cooking over medium heat for 8 minutes. Serve hot.

TOTAL CALORIES PER SERVING: 54   % OF CALORIES FROM FAT: 80%
PROTEIN: 1 gm   CARBOHYDRATES: 2 gm   FAT: 5 gm
CALCIUM: 75 mg   IRON: 1 mg   SODIUM: 386 mg   DIETARY FIBER: 3 gm

LEMON RICE SOUP

(Serves 6-8)

1 small onion or 3 scallions, chopped
1/2 head small cabbage, shredded
1/2 teaspoon garlic powder
1/8 teaspoon black pepper
1/8 teaspoon turmeric
2 Tablespoons oil
3 Cups pre-cooked rice
8 Cups water or vegetable broth
1/4 Cup lemon juice
1 Cup nutritional yeast
1 Tablespoon tamari or soy sauce

Saute onion or scallions, cabbage, and spices in oil for 5-8 minutes. Add rice, water or broth, lemon juice, yeast, and tamari or soy sauce. Simmer for another 10 minutes. Serve hot.

Variation: Instead of cabbage use 2 cups chopped fresh kale.

TOTAL CALORIES PER SERVING: 232   % OF CALORIES FROM FAT: 19%
PROTEIN: 11 gm   CARBOHYDRATES: 37 gm   FAT: 5 gm
CALCIUM: 82 mg   IRON: 5 mg   SODIUM: 212 mg   DIETARY FIBER: 2 gm

QUICK PEA SOUP

(Serves 4)

1 small onion, minced
1 Tablespoon oil
Salt and pepper to taste
two 10–ounce boxes of frozen peas
1 Cup soy milk
1 Cup pre–cooked rice or barley (optional)

Saute onion in oil over medium-high heat for 3 minutes. Add salt and pepper, and peas. Cook 5 minutes longer, stirring occasionally. Pour mixture into a blender. Add soy milk and blend until creamy. Pour blended mixture back into a pot. Reheat for a few minutes, adding pre-cooked rice or barley if desired. Serve hot.

TOTAL CALORIES PER SERVING: 162   % OF CALORIES FROM FAT: 31%
PROTEIN: 8 gm   CARBOHYDRATES: 21 gm   FAT: 6 gm
CALCIUM: 53 mg   IRON: 2 mg   SODIUM: 130 mg   DIETARY FIBER: 6 gm

CREAM OF CELERY SOUP

(Serves 3)

6 stalks of celery, chopped
1 small onion, chopped finely
1 Tablespoon oil
1/8 teaspoon pepper
1/4 teaspoon garlic powder
1 1/2 Cups soy milk
1/2 Cup water

Saute celery and onion in oil until onion is clear. Turn off heat.

Pour mixture into a blender. Add pepper, garlic powder, soy milk, and water. Blend until creamy. Pour mixture back into a pot. Reheat for a few minutes and serve hot.

TOTAL CALORIES PER SERVING: 138   % OF CALORIES FROM FAT: 53%
PROTEIN: 6 gm   CARBOHYDRATES: 12 gm   FAT: 8 gm
CALCIUM: 77 mg   IRON: 1 mg   SODIUM: 136 mg   DIETARY FIBER: 1 gm

CREAMY CAULIFLOWER SOUP

(Serves 4)

1 Cup water
1 head cauliflower, chopped
2 Cups water
1/2 Cup shredded coconut
1/2 teaspoon cinnamon
1/4 teaspoon nutmeg

Steam chopped cauliflower in 1 cup water over medium-high heat for about 12 minutes, until tender. Drain. Place half of the steamed cauliflower and coconut in a blender. Add 1 Cup of water to blender and cream mixture. Pour blended mixture back into a pot. Blend the remaining steamed cauliflower and spices with another cup of water. Add this mixture to the pot also. Reheat mixture over medium heat for 8 minutes and serve hot.

TOTAL CALORIES PER SERVING: 69   % OF CALORIES FROM FAT: 82%
PROTEIN: 1 gm   CARBOHYDRATES: 3 gm   FAT: 6 gm
CALCIUM: 13 mg   IRON: 1 mg   SODIUM: 7 mg   DIETARY FIBER: 2 gm

COLD TOMATO SOUP

(Serves 4)

6 Cups cold tomato juice
1 cucumber, finely chopped
2 scallions, finely chopped

2 stalks celery, finely chopped
2 ripe tomatoes, chopped
1/4 teaspoon cayenne pepper
1/2 teaspoon onion powder
1/2 teaspoon garlic powder
1 teaspoon basil

Mix all the ingredients together and serve chilled.

TOTAL CALORIES PER SERVING: 85   % OF CALORIES FROM FAT: 4%
PROTEIN: 4 gm   CARBOHYDRATES: 21 gm   FAT: <1 gm
CALCIUM: 58 mg   IRON: 3 mg   SODIUM: 1346 mg   DIETARY FIBER: 1 gm

CREAMY LENTIL SOUP

(Serves 4)

3 carrots, chopped
1 large onion, chopped
2 Tablespoons oil
1 1/2 Cups red lentils
4 Cups water
1 Tablespoon marjoram
Salt and pepper to taste
1 Cup water
Slices of lemon

Saute carrots and onion in oil over medium-high heat until onions are clear. Add remaining ingredients (except 1 cup water and lemon slices) and bring to a boil. Lower heat, but continue cooking over medium-high heat for 20 minutes. Pour mixture into a blender. Blend until creamy. Return mixture to a pot and add 1 cup of water. Reheat for a few minutes, until hot. Serve soup garnished with lemon slices.

TOTAL CALORIES PER SERVING: 289   % OF CALORIES FROM FAT: 24%
PROTEIN: 16 gm   CARBOHYDRATES: 42 gm   FAT: 8 gm
CALCIUM: 54 mg   IRON: 6 mg   SODIUM: 23 mg   DIETARY FIBER: 8 gm

ZUCCHINI/MUSHROOM SOUP

(Serves 6)

1 small onion, chopped
1 Tablespoon oil
3 or 4 medium zucchini, chopped
1/2 pound mushrooms, chopped
6 Cups water
1/2 Cup rolled oats
1/2 teaspoon salt (optional)
2 Tablespoons parsley, finely chopped

Saute onion in oil until clear. Add zucchini and mushrooms. Saute 5 minutes longer. Add water, oats, and seasonings. Simmer 12 minutes. Pour mixture into a blender. Blend until creamy. Return mixture to a pot and reheat. Serve hot.

TOTAL CALORIES PER SERVING: 84   % OF CALORIES FROM FAT: 34%
PROTEIN: 3 gm   CARBOHYDRATES: 12 gm   FAT: 3 gm
CALCIUM: 33 mg   IRON: 1 mg   SODIUM: 5 mg   DIETARY FIBER: 3 gm

Some readers will notice that a number of recipes in the Side Dishes section have a high percentage of calories from fat. In many cases the actual amount of fat in the recipe is quite low. When a recipe is low in calories, a small amount of fat will be a large percentage of calories. Because of the low amount of fat in many of these recipes, they can be classified as low to medium fat. Those wishing to reduce fat content further can use water in place of oil for sauteing.

SIDE DISHES

BROCCOLI SAUTE

(Serves 4)

1 pound broccoli (about 3 stalks), chopped
1 onion, chopped
1 1/2 teaspoons oil
1/2 Cup water
1 Tablespoon caraway seeds

Saute ingredients in a large frying pan over medium-high heat for 10 minutes.

TOTAL CALORIES PER SERVING: 54   % OF CALORIES FROM FAT: 30%
PROTEIN: 4 gm   CARBOHYDRATES: 8 gm   FAT: 2 gm
CALCIUM: 64 mg   IRON: 1 mg   SODIUM: 27 mg   DIETARY FIBER: 3 gm

CORN FRITTERS

(Serves 3-4)

1/2 Cup cornmeal
1/2 Cup cooked corn kernels
2/3 Cup whole wheat pastry or unbleached white flour
1/4 Cup cornstarch
2 Tablespoons tamari or soy sauce
Dash of pepper
2/3 Cup soy milk or water

Combine all the ingredients together, mixing well. Form 8 fritters and fry in a lightly oiled pan over medium-high heat until brown on both sides.

TOTAL CALORIES PER SERVING: 273   % OF CALORIES FROM FAT: 9%
PROTEIN: 9 gm   CARBOHYDRATES: 56 gm   FAT: 3 gm
CALCIUM: 34 mg   IRON: 2 mg   SODIUM: 804 mg   DIETARY FIBER: 3 gm

CAULIFLOWER AND CARROTS

(Serves 5)

1 head cauliflower, chopped
2-3 carrots, thinly sliced
1 1/2 teaspoons oil
1/3 Cup water
Juice from 1/2 lemon
1/2 teaspoon dry mustard powder
1/4 teaspoon tarragon
1/8 teaspoon pepper
Salt to taste

Steam cauliflower and carrots over boiling water for 10 minutes. Remove from heat. Add steamed cauliflower and carrots to remaining ingredients in a wok or skillet. Stir-fry over medium-high heat for 5-10 minutes.

TOTAL CALORIES PER SERVING: 36   % OF CALORIES FROM FAT: 38%
PROTEIN: 1 gm   CARBOHYDRATES: 6 gm   FAT: 2 gm
CALCIUM: 19 mg   IRON: <1 mg   SODIUM: 16 mg   DIETARY FIBER: 3 gm

STEAMED CAULIFLOWER WITH DILL SAUCE

(Serves 6)

1 head cauliflower, broken into flowerets
3 Tablespoons soy margarine
1 teaspoon dill weed
1 Tablespoon nutritional yeast
1/3 Cup water

Steam cauliflower over boiling water until tender. Meanwhile, melt margarine in a separate pan. Stir in dill weed, yeast, and water. Add steamed cauliflower and mix well before serving.

TOTAL CALORIES PER SERVING: 58   % OF CALORIES FROM FAT: 87%
PROTEIN: 1 gm   CARBOHYDRATES: 2 gm   FAT: 6 gm
CALCIUM: 11 mg   IRON: <1 mg   SODIUM: 69 mg   DIETARY FIBER: 2 gm

SWEET ORANGE RICE

(Serves 3-4)

1 Cup basmati rice
5 Tablespoons orange juice concentrate
2 1/2 Cups water
1/2 teaspoon cinnamon

Heat all the ingredients in a pot over high heat until the water begins to boil. Lower heat and simmer 15-20 minutes, until rice is done.

TOTAL CALORIES PER SERVING: 307   % OF CALORIES FROM FAT: 7%
PROTEIN: 5 gm   CARBOHYDRATES: 70 gm   FAT: <1 gm
CALCIUM: 37 mg   IRON: 2 mg   SODIUM: 7.5 mg   DIETARY FIBER: .8 gm

SEASONED RICE

(Serves 4-5)

1 Cup basmati rice
3 Cups water
1/4 Cup soy margarine
1/2 Cup water
2 Tablespoons nutritional yeast
Salt to taste
1/2 teaspoon garlic powder
1 teaspoon basil
10–ounce box frozen corn and/or peas (optional)

Cook rice in 3 cups water until done.

Melt margarine in pan and add 1/2 cup water, yeast, spices, and frozen vegetables. Heat for 5 minutes. Add cooked rice and heat 2 more minutes.

TOTAL CALORIES PER SERVING: 278   % OF CALORIES FROM FAT: 37%
PROTEIN: 5 gm   CARBOHYDRATES: 39 gm   FAT: 11 gm
CALCIUM: 28 mg   IRON: 2 mg   SODIUM: 139 mg   DIETARY FIBER: <1 gm

FRIED RICE

(Serves 4)

1 Cup basmati rice
3 Cups water
2 teaspoons oil
2 stalks celery, finely chopped
1 large green pepper, finely chopped
2 scallions, finely chopped
1 Tablespoon fresh ginger, grated
3 Tablespoons soy sauce or tamari

Cook rice in water until done.

When rice is cooked, add remaining ingredients and stir-fry over medium heat for 5 minutes.

TOTAL CALORIES PER SERVING: 206   % OF CALORIES FROM FAT: 11%
PROTEIN: 4 gm   CARBOHYDRATES: 41 gm   FAT: 3 gm
CALCIUM: 33 mg   IRON: 2 mg   SODIUM: 795 mg   DIETARY FIBER: 1 gm

LEMONY RICE

(Serves 4)

1 1/2 Cups basmati rice
4 Cups water
1/2 lemon

Bring water to a boil. Add rice. Squeeze lemon juice into pot, then put whole rind in the pot also. Cook until rice is done. Remove rind before serving.

TOTAL CALORIES PER SERVING: 254   % OF CALORIES FROM FAT: 1%
PROTEIN: 5 gm   CARBOHYDRATES: 57 gm   FAT: <1 gm
CALCIUM: 26 mg   IRON: 2 mg   SODIUM: 7 mg   DIETARY FIBER: <1 gm

ZUCCHINI PANCAKES

(Serves 4-5)

1 medium zucchini
1 small onion
1/2 Cup water
1 Cup whole wheat pastry flour
1/2 teaspoon garlic powder
1 Tablespoon parsley flakes
1 teaspoon tamari or soy sauce
2 teaspoons oil

Blend zucchini, onion, and water in a food processor. Pour into a bowl and add flour, garlic, parsley, and soy sauce. Form 10 small pancakes and fry in an oiled pan over medium heat. Brown both sides.

TOTAL CALORIES PER SERVING: 139   % OF CALORIES FROM FAT: 19%
PROTEIN: 5 gm   CARBOHYDRATES: 25 gm   FAT: 3 gm
CALCIUM: 29 mg   IRON: 1 mg   SODIUM: 89 mg   DIETARY FIBER: 4 gm

STEAMED SQUASH

2 yellow squash, thinly sliced
2 zucchini, thinly sliced
1 Tablespoon soy sauce or tamari
1 teaspoon nutritional yeast
1 teaspoon dill weed

Steam yellow squash and zucchini over water for 10-15 minutes (depending on how tender you prefer your vegetables). Remove squash and place in a dish. Sprinkle with soy sauce or tamari, nutritional yeast, and dill weed.

Variation: Stir in 1 cup croutons or vegan Chinese dry noodles before serving.

TOTAL CALORIES PER SERVING: 50   % OF CALORIES FROM FAT: 11%
PROTEIN: 3 gm   CARBOHYDRATES: 11 gm   FAT: <1 gm
CALCIUM: 48 mg   IRON: 1 mg   SODIUM: 264 mg   DIETARY FIBER: 4 gm

RED HOT ZUCCHINI

(Serves 3)

2 large zucchini, thinly sliced
2 small red hot peppers, minced
2 teaspoons oil

Stir-fry ingredients over medium-high heat for 5 minutes. Lower heat and cover pan. Continue to heat for 5 more minutes, stirring occasionally. Add a little bit of soy sauce for taste if desired.

TOTAL CALORIES PER SERVING: 66   % OF CALORIES FROM FAT: 46%
PROTEIN: 2 gm   CARBOHYDRATES: 9 gm   FAT: 3 gm
CALCIUM: 34 mg   IRON: 1 mg   SODIUM: 5 mg   DIETARY FIBER: 3 gm

ZUCCHINI, PEPPER, AND CORN

(Serves 4)

1 pound zucchini, chopped
1 small onion, chopped
1 large green pepper, chopped
1 Cup fresh or frozen corn
1/2 teaspoon parsley flakes
1/2 teaspoon onion powder
1/4 teaspoon pepper
2 teaspoons oil or 1/3 Cup water

Saute all the ingredients until vegetables are tender.

TOTAL CALORIES PER SERVING: 68   % OF CALORIES FROM FAT: 11%
PROTEIN: 3 gm   CARBOHYDRATES: 15 gm   FAT: 1 gm
CALCIUM: 31 mg   IRON: 1 mg   SODIUM: 136 mg   DIETARY FIBER: 4 gm

TOMATO/ZUCCHINI STIR–FRY

(Serves 5)

3 medium zucchini, thinly sliced
1 small onion, minced
3 medium tomatoes, chopped
1 Tablespoon garlic powder
2 Tablespoons basil
1/4 Cup nutritional yeast
Salt to taste
1 Tablespoon oil
1/2 Cup water

Stir-fry all the ingredients over medium-high heat until zucchini is tender.

TOTAL CALORIES PER SERVING: 89   % OF CALORIES FROM FAT: 33%
PROTEIN: 5 gm   CARBOHYDRATES: 13 gm   FAT: 3 gm
CALCIUM: 50 mg   IRON: 2 mg   SODIUM: 18 mg   DIETARY FIBER: 3 gm

CELERY SAUTE

(Serves 2)

5 stalks celery, chopped
1 1/2 teaspoons oil
1/3 Cup water
1 teaspoon tarragon
1 teaspoon soy sauce or tamari

Saute ingredients over medium-high heat for 3-5 minutes.

Variation: Use chopped bok choy instead of celery.

TOTAL CALORIES PER SERVING: 47   % OF CALORIES FROM FAT: 65%
PROTEIN: 1 gm   CARBOHYDRATES: 4 gm   FAT: 3 gm
CALCIUM: 37 mg   IRON: <1 mg   SODIUM: 259 mg   DIETARY FIBER: 2 gm

VEGETABLE MEDLEY

(Serves 4)

2 carrots, peeled and chopped
2 stalks celery, chopped
2 yellow squash, chopped
1 onion, chopped
1/2 pound mushrooms, chopped
1 1/2 Tablespoons oil
10–ounce box frozen peas
1 Tablespoon basil

Stir-fry carrots, celery, squash, onion, and mushrooms in oil for 5 minutes over medium-high heat. Add peas and basil. Heat for 5 minutes longer and serve.

TOTAL CALORIES PER SERVING: 163   % OF CALORIES FROM FAT: 33%
PROTEIN: 7 gm   CARBOHYDRATES: 24 gm   FAT: 6 gm
CALCIUM: 65 mg   IRON: 3 mg   SODIUM: 95 mg   DIETARY FIBER: 8 gm

CABBAGE, RAISINS, AND COCONUT

(Serves 4-5)

1 small cabbage, chopped
1 1/2 Tablespoons oil
1 Cup raisins

1/3 Cup shredded unsweetened coconut
1 teaspoon cinnamon

Heat ingredients over medium-high heat in covered pan, stirring occasionally, for about 12 minutes or until cabbage is tender.

TOTAL CALORIES PER SERVING: 235   % OF CALORIES FROM FAT: 36%
PROTEIN: 3 gm   CARBOHYDRATES: 40 gm   FAT: 10 gm
CALCIUM: 73 mg   IRON: 2 mg   SODIUM: 26 mg   DIETARY FIBER: 7 gm

CABBAGE/SPROUT SAUTE

(Serves 6)

1/2 head cabbage, chopped
1 stalk broccoli, chopped
Small onion, minced
1 Tablespoon oil
1/2 Cup water
1 teaspoon garlic powder
1 Tablespoon caraway seeds
1 pound mung bean sprouts
1 teaspoon soy sauce or tamari (optional)

Saute all the ingredients, except the sprouts and soy sauce, for 5 minutes. Add sprouts and saute for 5 minutes longer. Add soy sauce last if desired.

TOTAL CALORIES PER SERVING: 66   % OF CALORIES FROM FAT: 34%
PROTEIN: 4 gm   CARBOHYDRATES: 10 gm   FAT: 3 gm
CALCIUM: 48 mg   IRON: 1 mg   SODIUM: 19 mg   DIETARY FIBER: 2 gm

SWEET SAUTEED RED CABBAGE

(Serves 4)

1/2 red cabbage, shredded
1 apple, chopped

Small onion, chopped
1/2 Cup water
1/2 Cup raisins
1/2 teaspoon cinnamon

Use a non-stick pan, if possible, and heat ingredients, stirring occasionally, over medium-high heat for 10 minutes.

TOTAL CALORIES PER SERVING: 106   % OF CALORIES FROM FAT: 3%
PROTEIN: 2 gm   CARBOHYDRATES: 27 gm   FAT: <1 gm
CALCIUM: 50 mg   IRON: 1 mg   SODIUM: 16 mg   DIETARY FIBER: 5 gm

CREAMED MUSHROOMS AND SQUASH

(Serves 6)

1 pound mushrooms, sliced
2 small zucchini or yellow squash, finely chopped
Small onion, chopped
1 teaspoon dill weed
Salt and pepper to taste
1 Tablespoon oil
1/2 Cup water
1 1/2 Cups soy milk
2 Tablespoons whole wheat pastry or unbleached white flour
2 Tablespoons nutritional yeast (optional)

Stir-fry mushrooms, zucchini or yellow squash, onion, and spices in oil and water over medium-high heat for 10 minutes until squash is tender. Add soy milk, flour, and nutritional yeast. Stir until sauce is thick.

TOTAL CALORIES PER SERVING: 106   % OF CALORIES FROM FAT: 39%
PROTEIN: 5 gm   CARBOHYDRATES: 13 gm   FAT: 5 gm
CALCIUM: 44 mg   IRON: 2 mg   SODIUM: 38 mg   DIETARY FIBER: 3 gm

STUFFED MUSHROOMS

(Serves 2-3)

10 large mushrooms
1/3 pound yellow squash
1/3 small onion
1/2 carrot
1/8 teaspoon each garlic powder and pepper
1 Tablespoon oil

Remove stems from mushrooms. Chop stems, squash, and onion. Peel and grate carrot. Saute ingredients, except mushroom caps, over medium-high heat for 10 minutes, until squash is tender. Stuff mushroom caps with mixture. Heat stuffed mushrooms in oiled pan for 5 minutes over medium heat.

TOTAL CALORIES PER SERVING: 121   % OF CALORIES FROM FAT: 57%
PROTEIN: 4 gm   CARBOHYDRATES: 12 gm   FAT: 8 gm
CALCIUM: 30 mg   IRON: 2 mg   SODIUM: 14 mg   DIETARY FIBER: 3 gm

SAUTEED MUSHROOMS WITH FRESH PARSLEY

(Serves 4)

1 pound mushrooms
1 Tablespoon oil
1/2 Cup water
1 1/2 teaspoons garlic powder
1 Cup fresh parsley, chopped

Saute mushrooms in oil and water with garlic powder for 5 minutes. Lower heat and add chopped parsley. Saute another 5 minutes.

TOTAL CALORIES PER SERVING: 64   % OF CALORIES FROM FAT: 55%
PROTEIN: 3 gm   CARBOHYDRATES: 6 gm   FAT: 4 gm
CALCIUM: 25 mg   IRON: 2 mg   SODIUM: 11 mg   DIETARY FIBER: 3 gm

CURRIED CELERY AND MUSHROOMS

(Serves 4)

3 stalks celery, chopped
1 pound mushrooms, sliced
1 teaspoon oil
2 Tablespoons water
2 teaspoons curry powder
1/2 teaspoon garlic powder
1/8 teaspoon pepper
1/2 teaspoon salt

Saute ingredients in a large frying pan over medium-high heat for 10 minutes.

TOTAL CALORIES PER SERVING: 44   % OF CALORIES FROM FAT: 33%
PROTEIN: 3 gm   CARBOHYDRATES: 7 gm   FAT: 2 gm
CALCIUM: 18 mg   IRON: 2 mg   SODIUM: 306 mg   DIETARY FIBER: 3 gm

GOLDEN CHUTNEY

(Serves 6)

1 Cup dried figs, chopped
1 apple, chopped
1/2 lemon with seeds removed, chopped (including peel)
1/2 Cup molasses
1/4 Cup vinegar
1 teaspoon allspice
1/2 teaspoon cinnamon

Place ingredients in pot. Bring to a boil, then simmer for 25 minutes.

TOTAL CALORIES PER SERVING: 142   % OF CALORIES FROM FAT: 3%
PROTEIN: 1 gm   CARBOHYDRATES: 37 gm   FAT: <1 gm
CALCIUM: 117 mg   IRON: 2 mg   SODIUM: 12 mg   DIETARY FIBER: 3 gm

BOK CHOY STIR-FRY

(Serves 4)

2 bunches bok choy
2 teaspoons oil
1/2 teaspoon garlic powder
1 Tablespoon soy sauce
2 teaspoons sesame oil

Separate bok choy leaves and stems from one another, keeping stems. Chop stems. Heat oil over medium-high heat in a wok or large frying pan. Add bok choy stems and leaves and garlic powder. Stir-fry for 5 minutes. Lower heat and add soy sauce and sesame oil. Stir for 1 minute and serve.

TOTAL CALORIES PER SERVING: 72   % OF CALORIES FROM FAT: 60%
PROTEIN: 4 gm   CARBOHYDRATES: 5 gm   FAT: 5 gm
CALCIUM: 240 mg   IRON: 2 mg   SODIUM: 407 mg   DIETARY FIBER: unknown

BOK CHOY AND CARROTS

(Serves 4)

1 pound bok choy, chopped
1 carrot, peeled and very thinly sliced
1 teaspoon tarragon
2 teaspoons soy sauce or tamari
1 1/2 teaspoons oil
1/3 Cup water

Saute ingredients in oil and water over medium heat for 8-10 minutes.

TOTAL CALORIES PER SERVING: 39   % OF CALORIES FROM FAT: 44%
PROTEIN: 2 gm   CARBOHYDRATES: 5 gm   FAT: 2 gm
CALCIUM: 125 mg   IRON: 1 mg   SODIUM: 253 mg   DIETARY FIBER: unknown

BOK CHOY AND APPLE

(Serves 4)

1 pound bok choy, chopped
1 1/2 teaspoons oil
1/3 Cup water
1 apple, chopped
1 teaspoon ginger powder

Stir-fry ingredients over medium heat for 5 minutes.

TOTAL CALORIES PER SERVING: 52   % OF CALORIES FROM FAT: 38%
PROTEIN: 2 gm   CARBOHYDRATES: 8 gm   FAT: 2 gm
CALCIUM: 122 mg   IRON: 1 mg   SODIUM: 75 mg   DIETARY FIBER: unknown

BREADED OKRA

(Serves 3)

10–ounce box frozen okra (or fresh)
1/2 Cup water
1 teaspoon soy sauce or tamari
Pepper to taste
1/4 Cup corn meal
2 Tablespoons oil

Cook okra in water for 8 minutes. Remove from heat and drain. Sprinkle with soy sauce and pepper. Dredge okra in corn meal. Fry in oil over medium-high heat until brown on all sides (a few minutes).

TOTAL CALORIES PER SERVING: 156   % OF CALORIES FROM FAT: 55%
PROTEIN: 3 gm   CARBOHYDRATES: 16 gm   FAT: 10 gm
CALCIUM: 87 mg   IRON: 1 mg   SODIUM: 117 mg   DIETARY FIBER: unknown

EGGPLANT/OKRA DISH

(Serves 5)

Small eggplant, peeled and cubed
1 pound fresh okra, chopped
2 stalks celery, chopped
1 1/2 teaspoons oil
8-ounce can tomato sauce
1/2 teaspoon basil
Pepper to taste

Saute eggplant, okra, and celery in oil for 2 minutes. Add sauce and spices. Heat for 5 minutes longer, stirring occasionally.

TOTAL CALORIES PER SERVING: 96   % OF CALORIES FROM FAT: 42%
PROTEIN: 3 gm   CARBOHYDRATES: 13 gm   FAT: 5 gm
CALCIUM: 100 mg   IRON: 1 mg   SODIUM: 314 mg   DIETARY FIBER: unknown

STUFFED TOMATOES WITH MINTED RICE

(Serves 4)

1/2 Cup basmati rice
1 1/2 Cups water
4 ripe tomatoes
2 teaspoons dried mint
1/4 teaspoon salt

Cook rice in boiling water until done.

Carefully remove core and pulp from tomatoes. Then bake tomatoes at 400 degrees for 10 minutes. Remove from oven.

Add mint and salt to cooked rice, mixing well. Stuff tomatoes with rice mixture. Broil for 10 minutes and serve.

TOTAL CALORIES PER SERVING: 107   % OF CALORIES FROM FAT: 3%
PROTEIN: 3 gm   CARBOHYDRATES: 24 gm   FAT: <1 gm
CALCIUM: 17 mg   IRON: 1 mg   SODIUM: 150 mg   DIETARY FIBER: 2 gm

BROILED HERBED TOMATOES

(Serves 3)

3 tomatoes, cut in half
1 Tablespoon soy margarine
1 teaspoon basil
2 Tablespoons nutritional yeast
Dash of salt and pepper

Place margarine, basil, yeast, salt, and pepper on top of tomatoes. Broil for 4 minutes, until tops are slightly brown.

TOTAL CALORIES PER SERVING: 71   % OF CALORIES FROM FAT: 52%
PROTEIN: 3 gm   CARBOHYDRATES: 7 gm   FAT: 4 gm
CALCIUM: 21 mg   IRON: 2 mg   SODIUM: 60 mg   DIETARY FIBER: 2 gm

ORIENTAL–STYLE GREEN BEANS

(Serves 5)

1 1/2 pounds fresh green beans, snapped in half
2 teaspoons oil
3 cloves garlic, minced
1 teaspoon ginger powder

Stir-fry ingredients for 10 minutes over medium-high heat. Lower heat and if desired, add 1 Tablespoon sesame oil. Heat 2 more minutes until beans are tender, yet firm.

Variation: Add 1/4 cup pine nuts or almond slivers during last two minutes of heating.

TOTAL CALORIES PER SERVING: 54   % OF CALORIES FROM FAT: 33%
PROTEIN: 2 gm   CARBOHYDRATES: 9 gm   FAT: 2 gm
CALCIUM: 64 mg   IRON: 1 mg   SODIUM: 19 mg   DIETARY FIBER: 4 gm

MINTED GREEN BEANS AND BEETS

(Serves 4)

1 pound fresh green beans, snapped in half
4 fresh beets, peeled and thinly sliced
1/2 teaspoon dried mint
1 Cup water

Cook all ingredients together for 20 minutes over medium-high heat in covered pot.

TOTAL CALORIES PER SERVING: 45   % OF CALORIES FROM FAT: 4%
PROTEIN: 2 gm   CARBOHYDRATES: 10 gm   FAT: <1 gm
CALCIUM: 57 mg   IRON: 1 mg   SODIUM: 40 mg   DIETARY FIBER: unknown

SWEET AND SOUR CARROTS

(Serves 4)

1 pound carrots, thinly sliced
1 Tablespoon vinegar
2 Tablespoons water
2 Tablespoons molasses
1/4 teaspoon nutmeg
1/2 Cup raisins

Heat all the ingredients in a covered pan over medium heat, stirring occasionally, for 10 minutes.

TOTAL CALORIES PER SERVING: 135   % OF CALORIES FROM FAT: 2%
PROTEIN: 2 gm   CARBOHYDRATES: 34 gm   FAT: <1 gm
CALCIUM: 70 mg   IRON: 2 mg   SODIUM: 46 mg   DIETARY FIBER: 5 gm

SESAME CARROTS WITH DILL WEED

(Serves 4)

6 carrots, peeled and thinly sliced
2 Cups water
1 teaspoon dill weed
2 teaspoons sesame oil
2 teaspoons sesame seeds (optional)

Heat carrots in water for approximately 10 minutes over a medium-high heat in a large uncovered frying pan, until most of the water evaporates. Carrots will be slightly tender. Reduce heat to low. Add dill weed, sesame oil, and sesame seeds if desired. Heat 2 minutes longer and serve.

TOTAL CALORIES PER SERVING: 67   % OF CALORIES FROM FAT: 32%
PROTEIN: 1 gm   CARBOHYDRATES: 11 gm   FAT: 2 gm
CALCIUM: 29 mg   IRON: 1 mg   SODIUM: 38 mg   DIETARY FIBER: 3 gm

CREAMED SPINACH

(Serves 4)

10-ounce box frozen chopped spinach
1/2 Cup water
1 Cup soy milk

1 Tablespoon cornstarch
1/4 teaspoon nutmeg
1/2 teaspoon garlic powder
1 teaspoon soy sauce

Cook spinach in water over medium heat for 15 minutes. Add remaining ingredients and simmer over medium-low heat for 3 minutes longer, stirring often.

TOTAL CALORIES PER SERVING: 66   % OF CALORIES FROM FAT: 26%
PROTEIN: 5 gm   CARBOHYDRATES: 9 gm   FAT: 2 gm
CALCIUM: 121 mg   IRON: 1 mg   SODIUM: 177 mg   DIETARY FIBER: 2 gm

SAUTEED SPINACH WITH WATER CHESTNUTS

(Serves 3)

10-ounce bag fresh spinach, washed and chopped
1 Tablespoon oil
1/3 Cup water
2 cloves garlic, minced
1/2 teaspoon cumin
1/8 teaspoon cayenne pepper
1 Tablespoon lemon juice
4 ounces water chestnuts, thinly sliced

Saute all the ingredients over medium-high heat for 5 minutes.

TOTAL CALORIES PER SERVING: 104   % OF CALORIES FROM FAT: 42%
PROTEIN: 3 gm   CARBOHYDRATES: 13 gm   FAT: 5 gm
CALCIUM: 98 mg   IRON: 3 mg   SODIUM: 77 mg   DIETARY FIBER: 2 gm

CREAMED POTATOES, ONIONS, AND PEAS

(Serves 6-8)

2 pounds very small red or white potatoes, sliced thinly
6 Tablespoons soy margarine
6 Tablespoons whole wheat pastry or unbleached white
   flour
1 1/2 Cups soy milk
1 Cup water
2 teaspoons mustard
two 10-ounce boxes frozen pearl onions
10-ounce box frozen peas
Minced fresh parsley for garnish

Cook potatoes in boiling water for 15-20 minutes, until tender.

Meanwhile, melt margarine in a pan. Add flour, soy milk, and water. Stir until mixture thickens, about 2 minutes. Add mustard, salt, and pepper to taste. Add onions and peas and heat for 5 minutes longer, stirring often. Add potatoes and garnish with parsley.

TOTAL CALORIES PER SERVING: 367   % OF CALORIES FROM FAT: 33%
PROTEIN: 10 gm   CARBOHYDRATES: 54 gm   FAT: 14 gm
CALCIUM: 78 mg   IRON: 2 mg   SODIUM: 237 mg   DIETARY FIBER: 5 gm

STEAMED POTATOES WITH SAUTEED ONIONS

(Serves 4)

4 potatoes, peeled and thinly sliced
1 Tablespoon oil or 1/4 Cup water
1 large onion, chopped
1 teaspoon tarragon
1/4 teaspoon pepper

Steam sliced potatoes over boiling water until tender.

Saute onion and spices in a separate pot in oil or water over medium heat, until onions are transparent. Serve onions over potatoes.

TOTAL CALORIES PER SERVING: 157   % OF CALORIES FROM FAT: 21%
PROTEIN: 3 gm   CARBOHYDRATES: 29 gm   FAT: 4 gm
CALCIUM: 19 mg   IRON: 1 mg   SODIUM: 8 mg   DIETARY FIBER: 3 gm

SAUTEED COLLARDS AND TOMATOES

(Serves 4)

1 teaspoon oil
1 pound collards, chopped into bite–size pieces
2 ripe tomatoes, chopped
2 teaspoons lemon juice
1/2 teaspoon garlic powder
1/4 teaspoon mustard powder

Saute all the ingredients together over medium-high heat for 3-5 minutes. Serve hot.

TOTAL CALORIES PER SERVING: 38   % OF CALORIES FROM FAT: 36%
PROTEIN: 2 gm   CARBOHYDRATES: 6 gm   FAT: 2 gm
CALCIUM: 94 mg   IRON: 1 mg   SODIUM: 27 mg   DIETARY FIBER: 3 gm

MAIN DISHES

BROCCOLI AND CASHEWS OVER MILLET

(Serves 5)

2 Cups millet
6 Cups water
2 Tablespoons oil
2 teaspoons mustard seed
1 large bunch broccoli, chopped
1 onion, chopped
1/2 Cup water
1/2 Cup cashews, chopped
1 Tablespoon soy sauce

Cook millet in 6 cups of water in a covered pot over a medium-high heat for 15-20 minutes. The millet will become soft.

While the millet is cooking, heat oil in a large pan. Add mustard seeds and cover pan. As the seeds fry they will begin to pop (like popcorn). When you no longer hear any seeds popping (a minute or so), add the broccoli, onion, water, cashews, and soy sauce. Saute ingredients about 15 minutes until broccoli is tender. Serve sauted mixture over the cooked millet.

TOTAL CALORIES PER SERVING: 307   % OF CALORIES FROM FAT: 38%
PROTEIN: 9 gm   CARBOHYDRATES: 41 gm   FAT: 13 gm
CALCIUM: 66 mg   IRON: 4 mg   SODIUM: 312 mg   DIETARY FIBER: 9 gm

MEXICAN–STYLE CHICKPEAS

(Serves 3)

19-ounce can cooked chickpeas or garbanzo beans, drained (or 2 Cups pre-cooked chickpeas; fava beans can also be used)
1 large tomato, chopped
1/2 teaspoon garlic powder
1 1/2 teaspoons chili powder

Saute all the ingredients in a large frying pan over medium-high heat for 5 minutes. Add a little water, if necessary, to prevent sticking. Serve with rice or over a baked potato.

TOTAL CALORIES PER SERVING: 198   % OF CALORIES FROM FAT: 9%
PROTEIN: 8 gm   CARBOHYDRATES: 38 gm   FAT: 2 gm
CALCIUM: 54 mg   IRON: 2 mg   SODIUM: 482 mg   DIETARY FIBER: 7 gm

SPICY POTATOES, CABBAGE, AND PEAS OVER RICE

(Serves 4)

2 Cups rice
4 Cups water
5 medium potatoes, peeled, and thinly sliced
2 Cups water
1/2 green cabbage
10-ounce box of frozen peas (or equivalent fresh)
2 teaspoons curry powder
1 teaspoon turmeric
1/2 teaspoon ginger
1/2 teaspoon garlic powder
1/8 teaspoon cayenne pepper
Salt to taste (optional)

Cook rice in 4 cups water in a covered pot over medium-high heat until done.

In a separate frying pan, add sliced potatoes to 2 cups of water and heat over medium-high heat. Shred cabbage and add to potatoes. Add peas and spices to mixture. Continue heating in covered pan, stirring occasionally, until potatoes are tender. Serve over cooked rice.

TOTAL CALORIES PER SERVING: 547   % OF CALORIES FROM FAT: 1%
PROTEIN: 13 gm   CARBOHYDRATES: 121 gm   FAT: 1 gm
CALCIUM: 93 mg   IRON: 5 mg   SODIUM: 86 mg   DIETARY FIBER: 9 gm

CURRIED CHICKPEAS

(Serves 3)

Small onion, chopped
1 Tablespoon oil
19–ounce can chickpeas or garbanzo beans, drained (or 2
Cups cooked chickpeas)
1 Tablespoon curry powder
1/4 teaspoon black pepper

Saute onion in oil over medium-high heat for 3 minutes. Add chickpeas and spices and continue heating for 3 more minutes, stirring occasionally. Serve hot with rice and/or steamed kale.

TOTAL CALORIES PER SERVING: 239   % OF CALORIES FROM FAT: 24%
PROTEIN: 8 gm   CARBOHYDRATES: 38 gm   FAT: 6 gm
CALCIUM: 57 mg   IRON: 2 mg   SODIUM: 479 mg   DIETARY FIBER: 7 gm

VEGETABLE PANCAKES

(Serves 2)

2 Cups chopped vegetables (cabbage, scallions, carrots, celery, etc.)
1 Cup unbleached white flour
1 Cup water
1 Tablespoon soy sauce
1 teaspoon ginger powder (optional)
2 Tablespoons oil

Mix all the ingredients (except the oil) together in a large bowl.

Heat oil in frying pan over medium heat. Form six pancakes and fry in oil on both sides until brown. After frying pancakes, lay them on a paper towel for a few minutes to drain off excess oil.

TOTAL CALORIES PER SERVING: 441   % OF CALORIES FROM FAT: 29%
PROTEIN: 12 gm   CARBOHYDRATES: 68 gm   FAT: 14 gm
CALCIUM: 56 mg   IRON: 4 mg   SODIUM: 580 mg   DIETARY FIBER: 8 gm

CORN–STUFFED TOMATOES

(Serves 3)

6 large ripe tomatoes
1/4 Cup water
1 Cup frozen or fresh corn kernels
1/4 teaspoon cayenne pepper
1/2 Cup pitted black olives, chopped
1/2 Cup cornmeal
1/3 Cup water
2 Tablespoons molasses
1/2 teaspoon baking powder

Slice off tops of tomatoes and scoop out pulp and seeds.

Saute corn, pepper, and olives in 1/4 cup water over medium heat for 3 minutes.

Mix cornmeal, 1/3 cup water, molasses, and baking powder together.

Fill tomatoes with corn mixture. Cover tops of tomatoes each with 1/6 of the cornmeal mixture.

Broil tomatoes for ten minutes until the cornmeal topping becomes the texture of bread. Serve hot.

TOTAL CALORIES PER SERVING: 223   % OF CALORIES FROM FAT: 15%
PROTEIN: 6 gm   CARBOHYDRATES: 47 gm   FAT: 4 gm
CALCIUM: 82 mg   IRON: 3 mg   SODIUM: 345 mg   DIETARY FIBER: 8 gm

BLACK–EYED PEAS AND COLLARDS

(Serves 4)

1 1/2 Tablespoons oil
2 cloves garlic, minced
10–ounce box frozen black–eyed peas
10–ounce box frozen collard greens
1/4 Cup water
2 Tablespoons lemon juice

Simmer oil, garlic, peas, and greens together in a covered frying pan over medium-high heat for 10 minutes, stirring occasionally. Add water and simmer for 10 more minutes. Add lemon juice. Heat 2 more minutes. Serve hot with rice.

TOTAL CALORIES PER SERVING: 149   % OF CALORIES FROM FAT: 33%
PROTEIN: 7 gm   CARBOHYDRATES: 18 gm   FAT: 6 gm
CALCIUM: 79 mg   IRON: 3 mg   SODIUM: 50 mg   DIETARY FIBER: 6 gm

SPICY MILLET, CASHEWS AND PEAS

(Serves 4)

1 Cup millet
3 1/2 Cups water
10-ounce box frozen peas
1/2 teaspoon coriander
1/2 teaspoon cumin
1/2 teaspoon turmeric
1/2 teaspoon garlic powder
2 teaspoons soy sauce
2/3 Cup cashew pieces

Cook millet in water for 15 minutes over medium heat. Add remaining ingredients and continue cooking for 10 more minutes. Stir occasionally. Serve hot.

TOTAL CALORIES PER SERVING: 272   % OF CALORIES FROM FAT: 38%
PROTEIN: 9 gm   CARBOHYDRATES: 35 gm   FAT: 12 gm
CALCIUM: 30 mg   IRON: 4 mg   SODIUM: 365 mg   DIETARY FIBER: unknown

KAREN'S BULGUR CHICK

(Serves 4)

1 medium onion, chopped
4 cloves garlic, minced
1 Tablespoon oil
Pepper to taste
1/2 Tablespoon parsley flakes
2 1/2 Cups water
1 Carrot, grated
1 Cup bulgur (cracked wheat)
19-ounce can chickpeas or garbanzo beans, drained (or 2 Cups
    cooked chickpeas)

Saute onion and garlic in oil until onion is transparent. Add the remaining ingredients to pot, except chickpeas. Simmer 15 minutes covered. Add chickpeas and simmer 10 minutes longer. Serve hot.

TOTAL CALORIES PER SERVING: 335   % OF CALORIES FROM FAT: 14%
PROTEIN: 12 gm   CARBOHYDRATES: 61 gm   FAT: 5 gm
CALCIUM: 72 mg   IRON: 3 mg   SODIUM: 870 mg   DIETARY FIBER: 10 gm

FAVA BEAN DELIGHT

(Serves 3)

Small onion, chopped
1 Tablespoon oil
19–ounce can fava beans, drained
1 ripe tomato, chopped
Juice from 1/2 lemon
1 teaspoon cumin
1/8 teaspoon black pepper

Saute onion in oil until transparent. Add remaining ingredients and cook over medium heat, stirring occasionally, for 10 more minutes. Serve hot with rice.

TOTAL CALORIES PER SERVING: 182   % OF CALORIES FROM FAT: 25%
PROTEIN: 10 gm   CARBOHYDRATES: 26 gm   FAT: 5 gm
CALCIUM: 57 mg   IRON: 2 mg   SODIUM: 778 mg   DIETARY FIBER: 3 gm

BROCCOLI CHOW MEIN

(Serves 3)

3 stalks broccoli, chopped
1 Tablespoon oil
1/2 Cup water
1/2 pound mung bean sprouts

1/2 Cup slivered almonds or sunflower seeds (optional)
1 Tablespoon arrowroot starch or corn starch
1/2 Cup water
1 1/2 Tablespoons tamari or soy sauce
1 teaspoon sesame oil (optional)

Stir-fry broccoli in oil and 1/2 cup water for 3 minutes over medium-high heat. Add bean sprouts and almonds or seeds. Stir-fry for 2 more minutes.

Dissolve starch in 1/2 cup water. Add to broccoli and sprout mixture along with tamari or soy sauce and sesame oil if desired. Stir, then heat covered for 1 minute longer. Serve hot.

TOTAL CALORIES PER SERVING: 118   % OF CALORIES FROM FAT: 36%
PROTEIN: 7 gm   CARBOHYDRATES: 16 gm   FAT: 5 gm
CALCIUM: 89 mg   IRON: 2 mg   SODIUM: 554 mg   DIETARY FIBER: 1 gm

BROCCOLI STIR-FRY

(Serves 4)

1 bunch broccoli, chopped
1 carrot, thinly sliced
2 stalks celery, chopped
1 1/2 Tablespoons sesame seeds
1 Tablespoon oil
1/2 Cup water

Stir-fry ingredients over medium-high heat for 8 minutes. Serve with rice; this dish is especially good with the lemony rice recipe found on page 54.

TOTAL CALORIES PER SERVING: 91   % OF CALORIES FROM FAT: 50%
PROTEIN: 4 gm   CARBOHYDRATES: 9 gm   FAT: 5 gm
CALCIUM: 103 mg   IRON: 1 mg   SODIUM: 51 mg   DIETARY FIBER: 4 gm

SWEET SAUTEED CABBAGE

(Serves 4)

2 Tablespoons soy margarine
1 small cabbage, shredded
1/2 Cup raisins
2 teaspoons apple juice concentrate
1 teaspoon cinnamon
1 teaspoon caraway seeds

Saute ingredients over medium heat for 10-15 minutes until cabbage is tender. Serve hot over rice.

TOTAL CALORIES PER SERVING: 142   % OF CALORIES FROM FAT: 37%
PROTEIN: 2 gm   CARBOHYDRATES: 23 gm   FAT: 6 gm
CALCIUM: 62 mg   IRON: 1 mg   SODIUM: 87 mg   DIETARY FIBER: 6 gm

BOILED CABBAGE DISH

(Serves 4)

1/2 cabbage, shredded
2/3 Cup water
1 teaspoon oil
Small onion, chopped
1 tomato, chopped
1 teaspoon basil

Heat all the ingredients for 12-14 minutes over medium-high heat. Serve hot over pasta or rice.

TOTAL CALORIES PER SERVING: 39   % OF CALORIES FROM FAT: 32%
PROTEIN: 1 gm   CARBOHYDRATES: 7 gm   FAT: 1 gm
CALCIUM: 40 mg   IRON: 1 mg   SODIUM: 16 mg   DIETARY FIBER: 3 gm

SPICY RED LENTIL DISH

(Serves 3)

2 Tablespoons oil
1 Cup red lentils
1 onion, finely chopped
1 teaspoon cumin
1/4 teaspoon cayenne pepper
2 1/2 Cups water

Stir-fry lentils, onion, and spices in oil for 2 minutes. Add water and cook over medium heat for 15 minutes in covered pot. Stir occasionally. Serve hot with rice.

Variation: Brown lentils may be used. However, they take longer to cook.

TOTAL CALORIES PER SERVING: 264   % OF CALORIES FROM FAT: 33%
PROTEIN: 14 gm   CARBOHYDRATES: 32 gm   FAT: 10 gm
CALCIUM: 37 mg   IRON: 5 mg   SODIUM: 4 mg   DIETARY FIBER: 3 gm

FRIED EGGPLANT AND TOMATO STEW

(Serves 4)

1 1/2 pounds eggplant, peeled and sliced about 1/4" thick
6 Tablespoons oil
15-ounce can tomato sauce
1 teaspoon oregano
1/2 teaspoon garlic powder

Fry eggplant on both sides in oil in a non-stick frying pan. (An electric frying pan is great for this dish.)

Add sauce and spices. Heat for five minutes. Serve hot with rice or pasta.

CHINESE STIR–FRIED VEGETABLES AND PINEAPPLE

(Serves 4)

1 Tablespoon oil
1 Cup water
3 carrots, chopped
1 zucchini, chopped
6 ounces snowpeas (optional)
1/2 pound mushrooms, chopped
2 onions, sliced
2 large tomatoes, chopped
1/2 pound mung bean sprouts
10–ounce can crushed pineapple
3 Tablespoons soy sauce or tamari

Stir-fry all the ingredients together over medium-high heat until carrots are tender, yet crisp. Serve hot with rice.

Variation: Add baby corn and water chestnuts.

TOTAL CALORIES PER SERVING: 134   % OF CALORIES FROM FAT: 13%
PROTEIN: 6 gm   CARBOHYDRATES: 27 gm   FAT: 2 gm
CALCIUM: 56 mg   IRON: 3 mg   SODIUM: 807 mg   DIETARY FIBER: 6 gm

BEAN TACOS

(Serves 6)

2 Tablespoons oil
2 cloves garlic, minced
1 large onion, chopped
19-ounce can kidney beans, drained (or 2 cups of cooked
   kidney beans), mashed
1 Cup frozen or fresh corn kernels
1/4 teaspoon oregano
Salt and pepper to taste
Taco shells

Saute onion and garlic in oil. Add mashed beans and corn. Add spices and mix well. Heat 5-10 minutes over medium heat, stirring occasionally. Add water if necessary to prevent sticking. Serve in heated taco shells with shredded lettuce and chopped tomatoes.

TOTAL CALORIES PER SERVING: 198   % OF CALORIES FROM FAT: 34%
PROTEIN: 7 gm   CARBOHYDRATES: 28 gm   FAT: 7 gm
CALCIUM: 46 mg   IRON: 2 mg   SODIUM: 380 mg   DIETARY FIBER: 6 gm

PUMPKIN CASSEROLE

(Serves 5)

29-ounce can unsweetened pumpkin
2 apples, chopped
1 Cup raisins
2 teaspoons cinnamon
1/4 teaspoon nutmeg
2 Tablespoons molasses
1 Cup chopped walnuts

Preheat oven to 375 degrees.

Mix all the ingredients together and pour into a loaf pan. Bake at 375 degrees for 20 minutes. Serve hot.

TOTAL CALORIES PER SERVING: 361   % OF CALORIES FROM FAT: 37%
PROTEIN: 9 gm   CARBOHYDRATES: 57 gm   FAT: 15 gm
CALCIUM: 104 mg   IRON: 4 mg   SODIUM: 16 mg   DIETARY FIBER: 9 gm

RUTH'S TASTY SEITAN

(Serves 2)

8-ounce package seitan, thinly sliced
1 1/2 Tablespoons oil
1/2 teaspoon garlic powder
1/2 teaspoon onion powder
1/4 teaspoon paprika
1/4 teaspoon salt
Pepper to taste
1 Tablespoon whole wheat flour
1 Cup water

Heat seitan, oil, and spices over medium-high heat for 5 minutes, stirring occasionally. Add flour and water and heat for 2 minutes longer. Serve hot over mashed potatoes, rice, or pasta.

Variation: Substitute wheat gluten for seitan.

TOTAL CALORIES PER SERVING: 239   % OF CALORIES FROM FAT: 39%
PROTEIN: 21 gm   CARBOHYDRATES: 16 gm   FAT: 10 gm
CALCIUM: 23 mg   IRON: 4 mg   SODIUM: 277 mg   DIETARY FIBER: unknown

SEITAN SAUTE

(Serves 2)

2 Tablespoons oil
Small onion, minced
1 apple, diced
1/2 Cup raisins
8-ounce package seitan, cubed

Saute ingredients over medium heat for 5 minutes. Serve hot.

Variation: Substitute wheat gluten for seitan.

TOTAL CALORIES PER SERVING: 433   % OF CALORIES FROM FAT: 30%
PROTEIN: 23 gm   CARBOHYDRATES: 59 gm   FAT: 14 gm
CALCIUM: 55 mg   IRON: 5 mg   SODIUM: 8 mg   DIETARY FIBER: unknown

BREADED SEITAN

(Serves 3)

8-ounce package seitan, sliced
1/3 Cup nutritional yeast
1 teaspoon garlic powder
1/2 teaspoon cumin
1/2 teaspoon coriander
1/8 teaspoon pepper
2 Tablespoons soy sauce or tamari
2 Tablespoons oil

Combine the yeast and spices in a small bowl. Dip seitan in soy sauce or tamari, then in yeast/spice mixture. Fry in oil on both sides until brown over medium-high heat.

Variation: Substitute wheat gluten for seitan.

TOTAL CALORIES PER SERVING: 214   % OF CALORIES FROM FAT: 39%
PROTEIN: 20 gm   CARBOHYDRATES: 15 gm   FAT: 9 gm
CALCIUM: 45 mg   IRON: 5 mg   SODIUM: 362 mg   DIETARY FIBER: unknown

PASTA DISHES

CREAMED BROCCOLI AND PASTA

(Serves 5)

**1 pound pasta
4 stalks broccoli, chopped
2 Cups soy milk
1/2 Cup nutritional yeast
1/2 teaspoon basil
1/2 teaspoon onion powder
1/4 teaspoon black pepper
1 Tablespoon soy margarine
Salt to taste (optional)**

Cook pasta in water. Steam chopped broccoli in separate pot.

Mix soy milk, yeast, spices, and margarine together in a small pot. Heat over medium heat until mixture begins to bubble.

Drain pasta and mix with broccoli. Pour heated sauce over pasta and broccoli. Serve.

TOTAL CALORIES PER SERVING: 398   % OF CALORIES FROM FAT: 14%
PROTEIN: 20 gm   CARBOHYDRATES: 68 gm   FAT: 6 gm
CALCIUM: 140 mg   IRON: 6 mg   SODIUM: 123 mg   DIETARY FIBER: 10 gm

HEARTY MACARONI DINNER

(Serves 4)

2 Cups elbow macaroni
4 Cups water
1 onion, chopped
2 Tablespoons oil
3 Cups tomato juice
4 teaspoons chili powder
Salt and pepper to taste
10-ounce box frozen corn
19-ounce can kidney beans, drained (or 2 Cups cooked
    kidney beans)

Cook pasta in water until tender. Drain.

Saute onion in oil in a large pot. Add remaining ingredients, as well as cooked pasta. Simmer 15 minutes, stirring occasionally. Serve hot.

TOTAL CALORIES PER SERVING: 449   % OF CALORIES FROM FAT: 18%
PROTEIN: 16 gm   CARBOHYDRATES: 82 gm   FAT: 9 gm
CALCIUM: 66 mg   IRON: 4 mg   SODIUM: 1112 mg   DIETARY FIBER: 11 gm

BAKED BEAN AND PASTA CASSEROLE

(Serves 6)

19-ounce can pinto or kidney beans, drained (or 2 Cups
    cooked pinto or kidney beans)
3 Tablespoons molasses
Small onion, finely minced
4 Cups cooked pasta, drained
Dash of salt (optional)

Preheat oven to 350 degrees. Mix all the ingredients together. Pour into casserole dish and bake at 350 degrees for 15-20 minutes. Serve hot.

TOTAL CALORIES PER SERVING: 203   % OF CALORIES FROM FAT: 3%
PROTEIN: 8 gm   CARBOHYDRATES: 42 gm   FAT: 1 gm
CALCIUM: 60 mg   IRON: 3 mg   SODIUM: 295 mg   DIETARY FIBER: 6 gm

BROCCOLI PASTA DISH

(Serves 4)

2 Tablespoons oil
3 scallions, chopped
1-2 stalks of broccoli, chopped
1 Cup shredded cabbage
8 ounces elbow macaroni, cooked and drained
Small can black-eyed peas, drained
1 teaspoon sesame oil
Black bean sauce (optional)

Heat oil in a wok or large frying pan. Add scallions and broccoli. Saute until broccoli is tender, but crisp. Add cabbage, cooked pasta, and peas. Stir-fry five minutes. Add sesame oil and black bean sauce to taste. Stir for a few more minutes over heat. Serve hot.

Note: Black bean sauce can be found in Oriental grocery stores.

TOTAL CALORIES PER SERVING: 298   % OF CALORIES FROM FAT: 26%
PROTEIN: 10 gm   CARBOHYDRATES: 46 gm   FAT: 9 gm
CALCIUM: 60 mg   IRON: 3 mg   SODIUM: 35 mg   DIETARY FIBER: 6 gm

CHICKPEA SAUCE

(Serves 4)

**19-ounce can chickpeas or garbanzo beans, drained (or 2
    Cups cooked chickpeas)
15-ounce can tomato sauce
6-ounce can tomato paste
1 teaspoon onion powder
1 Tablespoon basil
Pinch of black pepper
Salt to taste**

Simmer ingredients for 5 minutes over low heat, stirring occasionally. When hot, pour over cooked spinach pasta or other type of pasta.

TOTAL CALORIES PER SERVING: 190   % OF CALORIES FROM FAT: 8%
PROTEIN: 8 gm   CARBOHYDRATES: 38 gm   FAT: 2 gm
CALCIUM: 60 mg   IRON: 3 mg   SODIUM: 1037 mg   DIETARY FIBER: 5 gm

CHICKPEA BALLS FOR PASTA

(Serves 3)

**19-ounce can chickpeas or garbanzo beans, drained (or 2
    cups cooked chickpeas), mashed
1/4 Cup whole wheat flour
1/8 teaspoon black pepper
1/4 teaspoon onion powder
1 stalk celery, finely chopped
2 Tablespoons oil**

Mix all the ingredients together in a bowl. Form 1 1/2" balls and fry in oil over a medium heat until brown on all sides. Serve with spaghetti and your favorite tomato sauce.

Variation: Serve chickpea balls by themselves as a side dish.

TOTAL CALORIES PER SERVING: 312   % OF CALORIES FROM FAT: 32%
PROTEIN: 9 gm   CARBOHYDRATES: 44 gm   FAT: 11 gm
CALCIUM: 60 mg   IRON: 3 mg   SODIUM: 491 mg   DIETARY FIBER: 7 gm

PASTA WITH SPICY TAHINI SAUCE

(Serves 5)

3 Tablespoons toasted sesame oil
1 Cup tahini (sesame butter)
3 Tablespoons lemon juice
1 1/2 – 2 teaspoons diced hot cherry peppers
1 1/2 teaspoons garlic powder
1 pound of pasta, cooked and drained

Mix together all ingredients (except cooked pasta).   Pour sauce over cooked pasta and serve.

TOTAL CALORIES PER SERVING: 509   % OF CALORIES FROM FAT: 42%
PROTEIN: 13 gm   CARBOHYDRATES: 65 gm   FAT: 24 gm
CALCIUM: 369 mg   IRON: 5 mg   SODIUM: 94 mg   DIETARY FIBER: 7 gm

BARBARA'S KALE CREAM SAUCE OVER PASTA

(Serves 5)

1 pound pasta, cooked and drained
1/4 Cup soy margarine

2 Tablespoons whole wheat flour
1 Cup soy milk
3 Tablespoons nutritional yeast
1/2–1 teaspoon each basil, thyme, dill, garlic powder
Salt and pepper to taste
10–ounce box frozen kale

Heat all ingredients (except pasta) together in pan over medium heat, stirring often, until kale is done. Pour sauce over cooked pasta and serve.

TOTAL CALORIES PER SERVING: 400   % OF CALORIES FROM FAT: 26%

PROTEIN: 13 gm   CARBOHYDRATES: 62 gm   FAT: 12 gm

CALCIUM: 88 mg   IRON: 4 mg   SODIUM: 150 mg   DIETARY FIBER: 4 gm

SOY PRODUCTS

Please note: Tofu has become a common food in the United States during the past decade. Most supermarkets now sell tofu. On the other hand, tempeh is still difficult to find in American shops. The best place to buy tempeh is in a natural foods store. Since tempeh can be stored in your freezer, you may want to purchase several packages once you have located some.

TEMPEH STROGANOFF

(Serves 4)

10–ounce package tempeh, cubed
1 carrot, thinly chopped
2 stalks celery, chopped
1 small onion, minced
1 Tablespoon oil
1/2 teaspoon basil
1/2 teaspoon garlic powder
1/2 teaspoon coriander
1/2 teaspoon cumin
1/8 teaspoon nutmeg
Salt to taste
2 Cups soy milk
2 Tablespoons nutritional yeast
2 Tablespoons whole wheat flour

Saute cubed tempeh, carrot, celery, onion, and spices in oil over medium-high heat until tempeh is lightly browned. Stir often while sauteing.

Lower heat to medium and add soy milk, yeast, and flour. Stir until a thick sauce forms and turn off heat. Serve hot over brown rice or pasta.

TOTAL CALORIES PER SERVING: 288   % OF CALORIES FROM FAT: 39%
PROTEIN: 21 gm   CARBOHYDRATES: 27 gm   FAT: 13 gm
CALCIUM: 134 mg   IRON: 3 mg   SODIUM: 99 mg   DIETARY FIBER: 2 gm

SWEET TEMPEH CABBAGE SAUTE

(Serves 4)

2 Tablespoons oil
10–ounce package tempeh, cubed
8 cabbage leaves, shredded
1 small onion, minced
3 ripe peaches, chopped

Saute all the ingredients over medium-high heat for 8 minutes. Serve hot.

TOTAL CALORIES PER SERVING: 239   % OF CALORIES FROM FAT: 46%
PROTEIN: 14 gm   CARBOHYDRATES: 22 gm   FAT: 12 gm
CALCIUM: 82 mg   IRON: 2 mg   SODIUM: 8 mg   DIETARY FIBER: 3 gm

TEMPEH BROCCOLI SAUTE

(Serves 4)

10–ounce package tempeh, cubed
2 stalks broccoli, chopped
1 small onion, minced
2 Tablespoons oil
2 teaspoons tamari or soy sauce (optional)

Saute cubed tempeh, broccoli, and onion in oil over medium-high heat until tempeh is lightly browned. Add soy sauce at last moment. Serve with brown rice.

TOTAL CALORIES PER SERVING: 227   % OF CALORIES FROM FAT: 48%
PROTEIN: 16 gm   CARBOHYDRATES: 18 gm   FAT: 12 gm
CALCIUM: 109 mg   IRON: 2 mg   SODIUM: 22 mg   DIETARY FIBER: 1 gm

TEMPEH/RICE POCKET SANDWICHES

(Makes 6 small pita sandwiches)

10–ounce package tempeh, cubed
1 onion, chopped
1 Tablespoon oil
1 1/2 Cups basmati rice
3 1/4 Cups water
1/2 Cup nutritional yeast
1/3 Cup whole wheat flour
1 Tablespoon garlic powder
1/4 Cup oil
1 2/3 Cups water
2 Tablespoons tamari or soy sauce
Pepper to taste
6 small pita bread pockets

Saute cubed tempeh and onion in 1 Tablespoon oil over medium-high heat until tempeh is lightly browned. Meanwhile, cook rice in 3 1/4 cups water in a separate pot until done.

To make a gravy, mix the yeast, flour, garlic powder, 1/4 cup oil, 1 2/3 cups water, tamari or soy sauce, and pepper together in a frying pan. Stir over medium heat for a few minutes until gravy thickens and is hot.

Mix the tempeh mixture and cooked rice together. Stuff into pita bread pockets. Pour gravy over tempeh/rice mixture and serve right away.

TOTAL CALORIES PER SERVING: 342   % OF CALORIES FROM FAT: 17%
PROTEIN: 18 gm   CARBOHYDRATES: 56 gm   FAT: 6 gm
CALCIUM: 90 mg   IRON: 5 mg   SODIUM: 364 mg   DIETARY FIBER: 1 gm

BARBECUED TEMPEH AND PEACHES

(Serves 4)

10–ounce package tempeh, cubed
2 Tablespoons oil
4 small ripe peaches, chopped
1 small onion, minced
8–ounce can tomato sauce
1/3 Cup vinegar
1/3 Cup soy sauce
1/4 teaspoon cayenne
1/2 teaspoon ginger
1 Tablespoon molasses

Preheat oven to 400 degrees. Saute cubed tempeh in oil over medium-high heat for 2 minutes. Add chopped peaches and onion. Saute 5 minutes longer. Mix tomato sauce, vinegar, soy sauce, spices, and molasses together. Pour tempeh/peach mixture into a casserole dish. Cover with sauce and bake for 20 minutes at 400 degrees. Serve hot.

Variation: Substitute 6 fresh apricots for the peaches and/or substitute 1 pound of tofu for tempeh.

TOTAL CALORIES PER SERVING: 288   % OF CALORIES FROM FAT: 39%
PROTEIN: 16 gm   CARBOHYDRATES: 34 gm   FAT: 12 gm
CALCIUM: 102 mg   IRON: 3 mg   SODIUM: 1749 mg   DIETARY FIBER: 4 gm

CURRIED TEMPEH AND RICE DISH

(Serves 3-4)

1 Cup basmati rice
2 1/2 Cups water
1 onion, chopped
2 Tablespoons oil
10–ounce package tempeh, cubed

1 Cup frozen or fresh peas
1 teaspoon tamari or soy sauce
2 teaspoons curry powder
1/2 teaspoon garlic powder
1/4 teaspoon black pepper

Cook rice in water until done. In a separate frying pan, saute onion in oil for 2 minutes. Add cubed tempeh, peas, tamari or soy sauce, and spices. Stir-fry for 8 minutes. Serve over cooked rice.

TOTAL CALORIES PER SERVING: 544   % OF CALORIES FROM FAT: 27%
PROTEIN: 25 gm   CARBOHYDRATES: 76 gm   FAT: 17 gm
CALCIUM: 129 mg   IRON: 5 mg   SODIUM: 173 mg   DIETARY FIBER: 4 gm

SCRAMBLED TOFU AND BOK CHOY

(Serves 4)

1 1/2 teaspoons oil
1/2 pound bok choy, chopped (stems and leaves)
12 snowpeas
Shake of black pepper
1 small onion, minced
1 teaspoon turmeric (optional)
1 pound tofu, crumbled
1 Tablespoon tamari or soy sauce

Saute all the ingredients except the tofu and tamari or soy sauce for 2 minutes over medium-high heat. Add the tofu and tamari or soy sauce and saute 2 minutes longer. Serve hot for breakfast or lunch.

TOTAL CALORIES PER SERVING: 124   % OF CALORIES FROM FAT: 53%
PROTEIN: 11 gm   CARBOHYDRATES: 6 gm   FAT: 7 gm
CALCIUM: 190 mg   IRON: 7 mg   SODIUM: 303 mg   DIETARY FIBER: unknown

TOFU/SQUASH SCRAMBLE

(Serves 2)

1 Tablespoon oil
1 medium yellow squash or zucchini, finely chopped
1/2 small onion, minced
1/4 teaspoon pepper
2 teaspoons basil
1/2 pound tofu, crumbled
1/4 teaspoon tamari or soy sauce (optional)

Saute all the ingredients except the tofu and tamari or soy sauce together over medium-high heat until the squash begins to soften. Add tofu and tamari or soy sauce and continue sauteing for another 3-5 minutes. Serve hot.

TOTAL CALORIES PER SERVING: 179   % OF CALORIES FROM FAT: 63%
PROTEIN: 11 gm   CARBOHYDRATES: 9 gm   FAT: 13 gm
CALCIUM: 151 mg   IRON: 7 mg   SODIUM: 11 mg   DIETARY FIBER: 3 gm

TOFU–STUFFED SNOWPEA PODS

(Serves 4-5)

1/4 pound snowpeas (about 30)
1/2 pound tofu, crumbled
1 teaspoon vinegar
2 Tablespoons water
1/2 teaspoon caraway seeds

Pinch off ends of snow pea pods. Slit pods open length-wise. Blend tofu with vinegar, water, and caraway seeds in a food processor until creamy. Stuff pods with tofu mixture and serve chilled.

TOTAL CALORIES PER SERVING: 58   % OF CALORIES FROM FAT: 43%
PROTEIN: 6 gm   CARBOHYDRATES: 4 gm   FAT: 3 gm
CALCIUM: 72 mg   IRON: 3 mg   SODIUM: 4 mg   DIETARY FIBER: unknown

TOFU–STUFFED CHERRY TOMATOES

(Serves 4)

1/2 pound cherry tomatoes
1/2 pound tofu, crumbled
1/2 teaspoon oregano
1/4 teaspoon garlic powder
1/4 teaspoon turmeric (optional)
Salt and pepper to taste

Remove stems from cherry tomatoes and carefully cut a small hole in the top of each tomato. Remove and save tomato pulp.

In a small bowl mix tofu, tomato pulp, and spices. Stuff cherry tomatoes with this mixture and serve chilled.

TOTAL CALORIES PER SERVING: 55   % OF CALORIES FROM FAT: 46%
PROTEIN: 5 gm   CARBOHYDRATES: 4 gm   FAT: 3 gm
CALCIUM: 65 mg   IRON: 3 mg   SODIUM: 8 mg   DIETARY FIBER: 2 gm

TOFU DILL DIP

(Serves 5)

1 cucumber, peeled
1 pound tofu, crumbled
1 teaspoon dill weed
2 Tablespoons lemon juice

1 Tablespoon dried parsley or 1/4 Cup fresh parsley, chopped
1/2 teaspoon garlic powder
Salt to taste

Place all the ingredients into a food processor or blender and blend until creamy. Serve with raw vegetables or crackers.

TOTAL CALORIES PER SERVING: 77   % OF CALORIES FROM FAT: 53%
PROTEIN: 8 gm   CARBOHYDRATES: 3 gm   FAT: 5 gm
CALCIUM: 104 mg   IRON: 5 mg   SODIUM: 8 mg   DIETARY FIBER: 1 gm

TOFU DIP

(Serves 5)

1 pound tofu, crumbled
1/4 Cup vegan eggless mayonnaise
1/2 teaspoon garlic or onion powder
1 Tablespoon tamari or soy sauce
1/4 Cup nutritional yeast
1/4 Cup water

Place all the ingredients together in a food processor or blender and blend until creamy. Serve with raw vegetables or crackers.

TOTAL CALORIES PER SERVING: 123   % OF CALORIES FROM FAT: 56%
PROTEIN: 11 gm   CARBOHYDRATES: 5 gm   FAT: 8 gm
CALCIUM: 112 mg   IRON: 6 mg   SODIUM: 256 mg   DIETARY FIBER: 1 gm

TOFU SPREAD

(Serves 7)

1 pound tofu, crumbled
1 small onion, chopped
1 carrot, grated
2 stalks celery, chopped
1/4 Cup tahini (sesame butter)
2 teaspoons lemon juice
Salt to taste (optional)

Place ingredients into a food processor or blender and blend for 2-3 minutes. Serve spread on whole wheat bread with lettuce or sprouts.

TOTAL CALORIES PER SERVING: 94   % OF CALORIES FROM FAT: 56%
PROTEIN: 7 gm   CARBOHYDRATES: 6 gm   FAT: 6 gm
CALCIUM: 142 mg   IRON: 4 mg   SODIUM: 35 mg   DIETARY FIBER: 2 gm

AVOCADO TOFU SPREAD

(Serves 4)

1 ripe avocado, peeled
1 ripe tomato
1/2 pound tofu, crumbled
1/4 teaspoon cayenne pepper
1/2 teaspoon onion powder
1/2 teaspoon garlic powder

Place all the ingredients in a food processor or blender and blend until creamy. Serve with raw vegetables or crackers.

TOTAL CALORIES PER SERVING: 131   % OF CALORIES FROM FAT: 72%
PROTEIN: 6 gm   CARBOHYDRATES: 6 gm   FAT: 11 gm
CALCIUM: 69 mg   IRON: 4 mg   SODIUM: 12 mg   DIETARY FIBER: unknown

TOFU MUSHROOM SAUCE

(Serves 5)

1 pound tofu, cubed or crumbled
1/2 pound small mushrooms
1 teaspoon garlic powder
1 teaspoon basil
1 Tablespoon oil
15-ounce can tomato sauce

Saute tofu and mushrooms with spices in oil for 5 minutes. Add sauce and continue heating 5 minutes longer. Serve hot over your favorite cooked pasta.

TOTAL CALORIES PER SERVING: 134   % OF CALORIES FROM FAT: 50%
PROTEIN: 10 gm   CARBOHYDRATES: 11 gm   FAT: 8 gm
CALCIUM: 113 mg   IRON: 6 mg   SODIUM: 572 mg   DIETARY FIBER: 8 gm

SPICY TOFU SAUTE

(Serves 4)

1/4 Cup water
1 Cup frozen or fresh corn kernels
1/2 Cup raisins
1 pound tofu, crumbled
1 teaspoon sesame seeds (optional)
1 Tablespoon tamari or soy sauce
1/4 teaspoon cayenne pepper

Saute all ingredients for 5 minutes over medium-high heat. Lower heat and cover pan. Allow to simmer a few minutes longer. Remove from heat and serve hot.

Variation: Stir in 1 Tablespoon sesame oil right before serving.

TOTAL CALORIES PER SERVING: 185   % OF CALORIES FROM FAT: 29%
PROTEIN: 11 gm   CARBOHYDRATES: 27gm   FAT: 6 gm
CALCIUM: 135 mg   IRON: 7 mg   SODIUM: 400 mg   DIETARY FIBER: 4 gm

TOFU "CODDIES"

(Serves 4)

1/2 pound tofu, crumbled
1 Cup water
2 potatoes, canned or boiled and peeled
1/2 Cup whole wheat pastry flour
1 Tablespoon tamari or soy sauce
2 Tablespoons Old Bay Seasoning
1 Cup wheat germ
2 teaspoons oil

Blend tofu, water, and potatoes in a food processor. Add flour, tamari and seasoning to blended mixture to form a stiff dough. Roll into patties and dredge in wheat germ. Fry in lighlty oiled pan until golden brown on each side. Drain on paper towels before serving.

TOTAL CALORIES PER SERVING: 234   % OF CALORIES FROM FAT: 28%
PROTEIN: 13 gm   CARBOHYDRATES: 34 gm   FAT: 7 gm
CALCIUM: 85 mg   IRON: 6 mg   SODIUM: 265 mg   DIETARY FIBER: 7 gm

TOFU SQUASH BURGERS

(Serves 3)

1/2 pound tofu, crumbled
1 pound yellow squash, grated
1/2 Cup toasted wheat germ
1/2 Cup whole wheat flour
1 small onion, minced
1 teaspoon tarragon
1 Tablespoon tamari or soy sauce
1/4 teaspoon pepper
1 Tablespoon oil

Mix all the ingredients (except oil) in a bowl. Form 6 patties and fry in oil over medium-high heat for 5 minutes until brown on one side. Turn and fry 5 minutes longer. Serve hot on whole wheat buns.

TOTAL CALORIES PER SERVING: 247   % OF CALORIES FROM FAT: 38%
PROTEIN: 14 gm   CARBOHYDRATES: 30 gm   FAT: 10 gm
CALCIUM: 135 mg   IRON: 7 mg   SODIUM: 353 mg   DIETARY FIBER: 8 gm

BROCCOLI AND TOFU SAUTE

(Serves 4)

2 Tablespoons oil
1 bunch broccoli, chopped (stems included)
1 inch ginger root, grated
2 cloves garlic, minced
3 scallions, chopped
1 Tablespoon vinegar
2 Tablespoons tamari or soy sauce
1 pound tofu, crumbled

Saute all the ingredients, except tofu, until broccoli is tender. Add tofu and stir-fry 5 minutes longer. Serve hot with brown rice.

TOTAL CALORIES PER SERVING: 190   % OF CALORIES FROM FAT: 58%
PROTEIN: 14 gm   CARBOHYDRATES: 11 gm   FAT: 12 gm
CALCIUM: 194 mg   IRON: 7 mg   SODIUM: 551 mg   DIETARY FIBER: 5 gm

SPICY SAUTEED TOFU WITH PEAS

(Serves 4)

2 pounds tofu, cut into small cubes
2 Tablespoons oil
1 teaspoon dill weed

1/2 teaspoon each basil, cumin, turmeric, and curry
2 cloves garlic, minced
2 Tablespoons tamari or soy sauce
1/4 Cup nutritional yeast (optional)
10-ounce box frozen peas, thawed
1/2 Cup cashew pieces (optional)

Stir-fry all the ingredients except the peas and cashews for 5 minutes over medium-high heat. Add peas and cashews and heat 5 minutes longer over low heat. Serve hot.

TOTAL CALORIES PER SERVING: 286   % OF CALORIES FROM FAT: 56%
PROTEIN: 22 gm   CARBOHYDRATES: 14 gm   FAT: 18 gm
CALCIUM: 261 mg   IRON: 14 mg   SODIUM: 580 mg   DIETARY FIBER: 6 gm

TOFU STEW

(Serves 4)

1 pound tofu, cubed in small pieces
1 1/2 teaspoons oil
1 small zucchini, chopped
1 carrot, peeled and sliced thinly
2 stalks celery, chopped finely
1 pound mushrooms, sliced
1/2 teaspoon garlic powder
Pinch black pepper
1/2 teaspoon oregano
1 small onion
1/2 teaspoon oil
3 Tablespoons whole wheat flour
1 Tablespoon tamari or soy sauce
1/4 teaspoon paprika
1 Cup water

Saute tofu, zucchini, carrot, celery, mushrooms, and spices in 1 1/2 teaspoons oil for 10 minutes over medium-high heat. Lower heat and simmer 5 minutes longer in a covered pan.

While tofu and vegetables are simmering, stir-fry onion in 1/2 teaspoon oil until clear. Add flour, tamari or soy sauce, paprika, and water. Stir until sauce begins to thicken. Add tofu and vegetable mixture to sauce. Stir well and serve hot.

TOTAL CALORIES PER SERVING: 224   % OF CALORIES FROM FAT: 52%
PROTEIN: 14 gm   CARBOHYDRATES: 18 gm   FAT: 13 gm
CALCIUM: 153 mg   IRON: 8 mg   SODIUM: 295 mg   DIETARY FIBER: 6 gm

TOFU CASSEROLE

(Serves 6)

2 Tablespoons oil
1 onion, chopped
1/2 pound mushrooms, chopped
1/2 pound zucchini, chopped
1 carrot, chopped
two 10-ounce boxes frozen spinach
1 teaspoon salt (optional)
1 teaspoon garlic powder
1 1/2 pounds tofu, crumbled
1/2 Cup nutritional yeast

Saute onion, mushrooms, zucchini, and carrot in oil over medium-high heat for 5 minutes. Add spinach and spices. Heat 10 minutes longer, stirring occasionally. Mix vegetables with crumbled tofu and yeast and continue heating for 5 minutes. Press into a casserole dish and serve warm.

TOTAL CALORIES PER SERVING: 199   % OF CALORIES FROM FAT: 44%
PROTEIN: 17 gm   CARBOHYDRATES: 17 gm   FAT: 10 gm
CALCIUM: 279 mg   IRON: 9 mg   SODIUM: 108 mg   DIETARY FIBER: 6 gm

TOFU ITALIANO

(Serves 4)

1 onion, chopped
2 Tablespoons oil
1 pound tofu, cubed
10-ounce box frozen corn
10-ounce box frozen peas
1/2 teaspoon oregano
1/2 teaspoon garlic powder
15-ounce can tomato sauce
1 Cup pitted black olives (optional)

Saute onion and tofu in oil over medium-high heat for 5 minutes. Add remaining ingredients and cook 10 minutes longer, stirring occasionally. Serve over your favorite pasta.

TOTAL CALORIES PER SERVING: 309   % OF CALORIES FROM FAT: 39%
PROTEIN: 16 gm   CARBOHYDRATES: 38 gm   FAT: 14 gm
CALCIUM: 159 mg   IRON: 9 mg   SODIUM: 773 mg   DIETARY FIBER: 8 gm

KAREN'S SLOPPY TOFU

(Serves 3)

1 small onion, chopped
4 cloves garlic, minced
1 Tablespoon oil
Pepper to taste
3 large mushrooms, chopped
1 carrot, grated (optional)
1/2 Tablespoon dried parsley
1/2 pound tofu, crumbled
2 teaspoons tamari or soy sauce (optional)
3 Tablespoons tomato sauce

Saute onion and garlic in oil until onion is clear. Add pepper, mushrooms, carrot, and parsley. Add tofu, tamari, and sauce. Cook, stirring occasionally, until heated through. Serve as a sandwich filling, sprinkled with nutritional yeast.

TOTAL CALORIES PER SERVING: 124   % OF CALORIES FROM FAT: 61%
PROTEIN: 8 gm   CARBOHYDRATES: 6 gm   FAT: 8 gm
CALCIUM: 98 mg   IRON: 5 mg   SODIUM: 107 mg   DIETARY FIBER: 1 gm

WAYNE'S TOFU CHILI

(Serves 8)

1 pound tofu, cubed in small pieces
2 Tablespoons oil
2 onions, chopped
3 green peppers, chopped
28-ounce can crushed tomatoes
15-ounce can black-eyed peas, drained
15-ounce can kidney beans, drained
15-ounce can white beans, drained
2 jalapeno peppers, minced
Garlic and chili powder to taste

Saute tofu in oil for 10 minutes. Add chopped onions and green peppers, and stir-fry 5 minutes longer. Lower heat. Add tomatoes, peas, beans, jalapeno peppers, and spices. Simmer for 12 minutes. You can add some tomato paste if sauce is too thin. You can also freeze the chili to serve later.

TOTAL CALORIES PER SERVING: 301   % OF CALORIES FROM FAT: 22%
PROTEIN: 19 gm   CARBOHYDRATES: 43 gm   FAT: 7 gm
CALCIUM: 164 mg   IRON: 8 mg   SODIUM: 413 mg   DIETARY FIBER: 10 gm

DESSERTS

Please note: The best dessert for people on a low-fat diet is fresh fruit. If you are looking for a low-fat dessert in this section choose Baked Papaya, Creamy Rice Pudding, Ginger Cookies or Chocolate Pudding. The remaining dessert recipes should be used on a limited basis.

HEAVENLY CHOCOLATE CUPCAKES

(Makes 18)

1 Cup molasses
1/2 Cup soy milk
2 Cups non-dairy, dark chocolate chips
6 Tablespoons soy margarine
1 teaspoon vanilla extract
4 Tablespoons cornstarch
2 Cups unbleached white flour
1 teaspoon baking soda
1/2 Cup soy milk

Preheat oven to 375 degrees. Combine molasses, soy milk, and chips in a small pan. Heat on low, stirring occasionally, until chips melt. Remove from heat and add margarine, stirring until it softens. Add vanilla and cornstarch to mixture and stir. Add flour, baking soda, and soy milk. Mix ingredients well.

Lightly oil 18 muffin cups and divide the batter among them, filling each cup about half full. Bake 20 minutes at 375 degrees. Cool cupcakes before removing from tins.

Variations: Replace chocolate chips with non-dairy carob chips or add 3/4 cup chopped walnuts to batter before baking.

TOTAL CALORIES PER SERVING: 231   % OF CALORIES FROM FAT: 43%
PROTEIN: 3 gm   CARBOHYDRATES: 34 gm   FAT: 11 gm
CALCIUM: 65 mg   IRON: 2 mg   SODIUM: 119 mg   DIETARY FIBER: <1 gm

GINGER COOKIES

(Makes 2 dozen)

1/4 Cup soy margarine
1/4 Cup molasses
1 1/2 Cups whole wheat pastry flour
1 teaspoon baking soda
1/2 teaspoon ginger powder
1/2 teaspoon cinnamon
1/4 teaspoon ground cloves

Preheat oven to 375 degrees. Mash soy margarine with a fork in a bowl. Add the remaining ingredients and stir well.

Form two dozen 1" round balls and place on a lightly oiled cookie sheet. Bake for 12 to 15 minutes at 375 degrees.

Remove cookies from the oven and allow to cool before removing from the cookie sheet.

TOTAL CALORIES PER COOKIE: 49   % OF CALORIES FROM FAT: 37%
PROTEIN: 1 gm   CARBOHYDRATES: 7 gm   FAT: 2 gm
CALCIUM: 13 mg   IRON: <1 mg   SODIUM: 70 mg   DIETARY FIBER: <1 gm

CAROB CHIP COOKIES

(Makes 2 dozen)

2/3 Cup water
2 Cups whole wheat flour
1 teaspoon baking soda
2 teaspoons vanilla extract
1/2 Cup oil or soy margarine
1/2 Cup raisins
1/2 Cup peanuts
1/2 Cup non-dairy carob chips

Preheat oven to 375 degrees. Mix all the ingredients together in a large bowl. Spoon batter onto a lightly oiled cookie sheet, forming 24 cookies.

Bake 12-15 minutes at 375 degrees. Allow cookies to cool before removing from the cookie sheet.

TOTAL CALORIES PER COOKIE: 119   % OF CALORIES FROM FAT: 57%
PROTEIN: 2 gm   CARBOHYDRATES: 12 gm   FAT: 8 gm
CALCIUM: 9 mg   IRON: 1 mg   SODIUM: 48 mg   DIETARY FIBER: 2 gm

FESTIVE CASHEW COOKIES

(Makes 2 dozen)

2 Cups raw cashews
1 Cup rolled oats
1 teaspoon cinnamon
1/3 Cup molasses or maple syrup
1/2 Cup water
1/4 Cup oil
1 teaspoon vanilla extract
Small jar of unsweetened jam

Preheat oven to 375 degrees. Grind the raw cashews and rolled oats together in a food processor for a few minutes. Pour mixture into a large bowl and add the remaining ingredients, except the jam. Mix all the ingredients together.

Form 24 round balls and place on a lightly oiled cookie sheet. With your thumb, form a small well in the center of each ball. Place a small amount of jam in each well.

Bake for 15 minutes at 375 degrees. Allow cookies to cool before removing them from the cookie sheet. These cookies make a wonderful gift.

TOTAL CALORIES PER COOKIE: 125   % OF CALORIES FROM FAT: 55%
PROTEIN: 2 gm   CARBOHYDRATES: 13 gm   FAT: 8 gm
CALCIUM: 20 mg   IRON: 1 mg   SODIUM: 71 mg   DIETARY FIBER: 1 gm

CAROB RAISIN PEANUT CLUSTERS

(Makes 2 dozen)

3 Cups non-dairy carob chips
1/2 Cup raisins
1/2 Cup shelled peanuts

Melt carob chips in a double boiler over medium heat. Add raisins and peanuts. Remove pot from stove and mix ingredients together.

Drop by spoonfuls onto a cookie sheet, forming two dozen clusters. Cool in refrigerator for at least 15 minutes and serve.

Variation: Substitute non-dairy dark chocolate chips for carob chips and/or substitute other dried fruit for the raisins and different nuts for the peanuts.

TOTAL CALORIES PER CLUSTER: 135   % OF CALORIES FROM FAT: 61%
PROTEIN: 2 gm   CARBOHYDRATES: 15 gm   FAT: 9 gm
CALCIUM: 10 mg   IRON: 1 mg   SODIUM: 1 mg   DIETARY FIBER: 2 gm

CAKE-LIKE CHOCOLATE CHIP COOKIES

(Makes 2 dozen)

12-ounce package of non-dairy, dark chocolate chips
1 teaspoon baking soda
2 1/4 Cups whole wheat flour
1 1/2 teaspoons vanilla extract
1 large banana, mashed
1/4 Cup maple syrup
1/2 Cup water

Preheat oven to 375 degrees. Mix all the ingredients together in a bowl. Form 24 cookies on a lightly oiled cookie sheet.

Bake for 8-10 minutes at 375 degrees. Cool cookies before removing from the cookie sheet.

Variation: Add 1/2 cup chopped nuts to the batter before baking.

TOTAL CALORIES PER COOKIE: 122   % OF CALORIES FROM FAT: 39%
PROTEIN: 2 gm   CARBOHYDRATES: 19 gm   FAT: 5 gm
CALCIUM: 10 mg   IRON: 1 mg   SODIUM: 48 mg   DIETARY FIBER: 1 gm

BAKED PAPAYA

(Serves 4)

**2 ripe papayas
4 Tablespoons frozen orange juice concentrate
1/2 teaspoon cinnamon**

Preheat oven to 350 degrees. Remove skin from both papayas. Slice papayas and lay fruit in a baking dish. Sprinkle papaya with dabs of the frozen juice concentrate and cinnamon.

Bake for 20-25 minutes at 350 degrees. Serve hot.

TOTAL CALORIES PER SERVING: 88   % OF CALORIES FROM FAT: 2%
PROTEIN: 1 gm   CARBOHYDRATES: 22 gm   FAT: <1 gm
CALCIUM: 42 mg   IRON: <1 mg   SODIUM: 5 mg   DIETARY FIBER: 1 gm

BAKED PEARS IN BLANKETS

(Serves 4)

2 ripe pears
1/2 teaspoon cinnamon
1/4 teaspoon nutmeg
1/2 Cup soy margarine
1 1/2 Cups unbleached white flour
1/4 Cup cold water
3 Tablespoons molasses
2 Tablespoons soy margarine, melted

Preheat oven to 425 degrees. Slice each pear into 8 wedges and place them in a bowl. Sprinkle pears with cinnamon and nutmeg.

In a separate bowl, mash 1/2 cup soy margarine with a fork. Add the flour, cold water, and molasses. Mix ingredients well to form a soft dough. Roll dough out on a floured board. Cut into 16 long strips. Wrap each pear wedge with the dough and place it on a lightly oiled cookie sheet.

Brush each pear wedge with the 2 Tablespoons melted margarine. Bake for 25 minutes at 425 degrees. Serve warm. Friends would enjoy these at a party.

TOTAL CALORIES PER SERVING: 489   % OF CALORIES FROM FAT: 52%
PROTEIN: 5 gm   CARBOHYDRATES: 55 gm   FAT: 28.5 gm
CALCIUM: 70 mg   IRON: 3 mg   SODIUM: 331 mg   DIETARY FIBER: 4 gm

PUMPKIN PIE

(Makes 2 pies -- Serves 12)

1 1/2 Cups soymilk
2 Tablespoons Ener-G Egg Replacer
16-ounce can pumpkin (with no added sugar)
1/2 Cup maple syrup
1 teaspoon cinnamon
1/2 teaspoon ginger
2 vegan pie crusts

Preheat oven to 425 degrees. Blend the soymilk and Ener-G Egg Replacer together in a bowl using a whisk. Add the remaining ingredients and mix well.

Pour into two pre-made vegan pie crusts (available at some natural foods stores and supermarkets). Bake 20 minutes at 425 degrees. Remove pies from the oven and allow to cool before slicing and serving.

TOTAL CALORIES PER SERVING: 221   % OF CALORIES FROM FAT: 45%
PROTEIN: 4 gm   CARBOHYDRATES: 28 gm   FAT: 11 gm
CALCIUM: 47 mg   IRON: 2 mg   SODIUM: 202 mg   DIETARY FIBER: 1 gm (filling only)

SOY WHIPPED CREAM

(makes enough to top one pie)

1/4 Cup soy milk
1/2 Cup oil
1 Tablespoon maple syrup
1/2 teaspoon vanilla extract

Place soy milk and 1/4 cup oil in a blender. Blend at highest speed and slowly drizzle in remaining 1/4 cup oil. Blend in syrup and vanilla. Add a little more oil if necessary to thicken. Chill and serve.

Note: This recipe does not work well on damp, rainy days.

TOTAL CALORIES PER SERVING (1/6 of recipe): 175   % OF CALORIES FROM FAT: 95%
PROTEIN: <1 gm   CARBOHYDRATES: 3 gm   FAT: 18 gm
CALCIUM: 4 mg   IRON: <1 mg   SODIUM: 5 mg   DIETARY FIBER: 0 gm

CHOCOLATE PUDDING

(Serves 3)

1 1/2 Cups soy milk

3 Tablespoons cornstarch
1/4 teaspoon vanilla
1/4 Cup maple syrup
1/4 Cup cocoa powder
2 bananas, sliced (optional)

Whisk all the ingredients (except the bananas) together in a pot. Cook over medium heat, stirring constantly until pudding thickens.

Remove pot from stove. Stir in sliced bananas if desired. Chill for at least 15 minutes before serving.

Variation: Replace chocolate powder with non-dairy carob powder.

TOTAL CALORIES PER SERVING: 198   % OF CALORIES FROM FAT: 17%
PROTEIN: 7 gm   CARBOHYDRATES: 36 gm   FAT: 4 gm
CALCIUM: 92 mg   IRON: 1 mg   SODIUM: 155 mg   DIETARY FIBER: negligible

KAREN'S CREAMY RICE PUDDING

(Serves 8)

2 Cups pre-cooked rice
1 1/2 teaspoons cinnamon
1 Tablespoon vanilla extract
1 Cup raisins
1/2 Cup slivered almonds (optional)
3-4 Cups soy milk

Mix all the ingredients together in a pot. Simmer until the mixture begins to thicken (15-20 minutes), stirring occasionally.

Remove from stove and serve hot or cold.

TOTAL CALORIES PER SERVING: 175   % OF CALORIES FROM FAT: 14%
PROTEIN: 5 gm   CARBOHYDRATES: 34 gm   FAT: 3 gm
CALCIUM: 47 mg   IRON: 1.5 mg   SODIUM: 53 mg   DIETARY FIBER: 2 gm

FOOD DEFINITIONS AND ORIGINS

ALMONDS are nuts found in the fruit of a small tree known as *Prunus amygdalus*. No one knows exactly where the almond originated, but *Prunus ulmifolia*, the wild species from China contributed to our present day nut. When blended with water and strained, almonds make an excellent nut milk.

APPLES are firm, rounded fruits of the tree *Pyrus malus*, which grows in temperate regions. There are about 7,500 different types of apples worldwide, including 2,500 varieties in the United States alone. The majority of commercially grown apple crops in this country consist of eighteen to twenty-five varieties. "Delicious" is the most common. The skin of the apple is usually red, but may be yellow or green. Apples are high in fiber.

ARROWROOT is a fine white powdery substance that comes from a tropical plant and can be used to thicken gravies, soups, and fruit compotes. It also is called arrowroot starch, arrowroot flour, and arrowroot powder. It is used in much the same way that cornstarch is used and is found commonly in Oriental shops.

AVOCADOS are oval - or pear - shaped fruits that grow on a tropical American tree known as *Persea americana*. They have a leathery green or blackish skin, a large seed, and bland, yellowish-green edible pulp. Avocados are native to Central America. They are also called alligator pears.

BANANAS are crescent-shaped fruits grown on several treelike tropical or subtropical plants of the genus *Musa*. The most widely cultivated banana grows on *Musa sapientum*, a plant which has long broad leaves and hanging clusters of fruit. The edible part of a banana consists of a white, pulpy flesh. The flesh is surrounded by a yellow or reddish skin, which can be peeled away easily. Bananas are high in potassium. They originated over 4,000 years ago in Malaysia.

BEETS are fleshy, dark red roots that are eaten as a vegetable. They grow on any of several widely cultivated plants of the genus *Beta*, especially *Beta vulgaris*. The leaves can be eaten as greens.

BELL PEPPERS are mild-flavored, bell-shaped fruits of the plant *Capisicum frutescens grossum*, which is native to Latin America. Bell peppers are red when ripe, but often are eaten when green. They are also called sweet peppers. Bell peppers are rich in vitamin C.

BLACK–EYED PEAS are the seeds of cowpeas. They are white with a black spot and look more like a bean than a pea. Black-eyed peas traditionally are eaten in the southeastern United States on New Year's Day. They are sometimes called "soul food."

BLUEBERRIES are small berries that grow on any of several North American shrubs of the genus *Vaccinium*. The shrubs flower before producing berries. The fruit is blue, purplish, or blackish, and very sweet when ripe. Wild blueberry bushes can be found along hiking trails in the mountains. The berries produced on these bushes tend to be smaller and not as sweet.

BOK CHOY is an Oriental vegetable that is similar to, but milder in taste than, cabbage. Bok choy has snow-white stalks, a slightly bulbous base, and dark green leaves. Hong Kong farmers alone grow over twenty varieties of *Brassica chinensis*. In the United States four or five kinds are available. Bok choy sum or choy sum is almost identical to bok choy, but has yellow flowers. It is slightly smaller with narrower stalks. Bok choy sum also has green leaves, which are a shade lighter. Shanghai bok choy has spoon-shaped leaves and stems that are flatter than regular bok choy. Shanghai bok choy has light green leaves and is picked at a smaller size than bok choy. Taiwan bok choy is a yellowish green color and has broad delicate leaves that are almost lettuce-like in texture. Bok choy can be used in place of cabbage or even celery in some dishes.

BROCCOLI is the flower of the plant, *Brassica oleracea italica*. The plant is derived from wild cabbage. The flower is eaten as a vegetable before the green, tightly clustered buds have opened. Broccoli is high in vitamin C and a good source of calcium.

BULGUR is the bran and germ of wheat grain. It is also called cracked wheat. Bulgur is to the Middle East what rice is to the Orient and kasha is to Russia. It can be used in salads or in place of rice. Bulgur can be added to spaghetti sauce to thicken it.

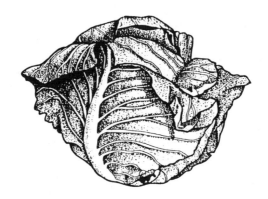

CABBAGES are plants, *Brassica oleracea capitata*, which grow in temperate climates throughout the world. They have a short, thick stalk, and a large head formed by tightly overlapping green or reddish leaves. The Italians developed the popular savoy cabbage.

CANTALOUPES are a variety of melon known as *Cucumis melo cantalupensis*, which has ribbed fruit with a rough rind and an aromatic orange flesh. In the United States canteloupes are also known as muskmelons or *Cucumis melo reticulatus*.

CARROTS are the long, tapering yellow-orange roots of the widely cultivated plant, *Dacus carota sativa*. The plant has finely divided leaves and white flowers. This vegetable is native to the Near East and Central Asia. In its ancient form the edible root was purple, not orange. Carrots are high in vitamin A.

CASHEWS are kidney-shaped nuts that grow on tropical evergreen trees known as *Anacardium occidentale*. Cashews actually are the seed of the cashew fruit, which is a fleshy, pear-shaped "apple." The seed (nut) hangs from the outside end of the fruit. The tree is native to coastal areas of northeastern Brazil. Cashews are the fifth leading nut crop in the world.

CAULIFLOWER is a compact whitish flower head of the plant *Brassica oleracea botrytis*. It is related to cabbage and broccoli and is derived from wild cabbage plants. Cauliflower is an excellent source of vitamin C.

CELERY is the stalk of the plant *Apium graveolens dulce*, which is native to Europe and Asia. Its small seeds, celery seeds, are used as seasoning. Celery is the third leading salad crop in the United States. It is derived from wild celery, which had more leaves.

CHICKPEAS are seeds. They grow on a bushy plant known as *Cicer arietenum* in the Mediterranean region and Central Asia. They also are called garbanzo beans. Eighty-seven percent of chickpeas are produced in India and Pakistan.

CHINESE BROCCOLI is an Oriental vegetable with smooth, round, green stems and has larger leaves than western broccoli. The Latin name for Chinese broccoli is *Brassica alboglabra*. It is also called Chinese kale and Gai lan in Cantonese. Chinese broccoli has a cluster of white flowers on the stem and can be used in place of western broccoli in many dishes. Chinese broccoli is high in calcium.

CHINESE CABBAGE is the most important leafy vegetable of northern China. The Latin name for Chinese cabbage is *Brassica perkinensis*. It is also called napa cabbage, celery cabbage, Hakusai in Japanese, and Wong nga bok choy or wong bok in Cantonese. Chinese cabbage can be used in place of western cabbage in most recipes.

COCONUT is the fruit of the coconut palm. The seed of the fruit is large, with a thick, hard shell that encloses edible white meat. The center of the seed is filled with a milky liquid. The liquid is known as coconut milk. Coconut can be eaten fresh or dried and grated. It is high in fat and should be used only in small quantities.

COLLARD GREENS are large, dark green leaves grown on a variety of the kale plant known as *Brassica oleracea acephala*. Collards are grown mostly in the southeastern United States. They are high in calcium.

CORN is a tall, widely cultivated cereal plant known as *Zea mays*. The plant bears seeds or kernels on large ears. There are several different varieties of corn. Corn is indigenous to the United States and is sometimes called Indian corn or maize.   In England "corn" refers to wheat and in Scotland and Ireland, corn refers to oats.

CORNMEAL can be white or yellow. White cornmeal is milled from white corn and yellow cornmeal is milled from yellow corn. Cornmeal is more coarse in texture than flour. It can be used in baking or as a hot cereal.

CUCUMBERS are cylindrical fruits which grow on the vine known as *Cucumis sativus*. The fruit has a hard green rind and white succulent flesh. China is the largest producer of cucumbers.

DATES are sweet, oblong fruits of the date palm. They contain a narrow hard seed. Unlike most fruits, dates do not contain any vitamin C. Dates grow on what is called the Tree of Life and grew in the Holy Land at least 8,000 years ago. They grow in clusters of up to 200 dates weighing up to 25 pounds. They rank among the top twenty fruits of the world. Today Egypt is the biggest producer of dates.

EGGPLANT is an ovoid fruit which has a glossy, dark, purple skin. It grows on the tropical Old World plant *Solanum melongena*. When cooked, eggplant is eaten as a vegetable. Eggplants are used widely in Greek, Italian, and Middle Eastern cooking. They are also known as aubergines.

FAVA BEANS resemble lima beans, but are slightly larger. Fava beans also are known as horse beans and broad beans. This legume is referred to in the Bible and was consumed throughout the Old World. Fava beans are native to northern Africa and the eastern Mediterranean region. The Chinese used fava beans 5,000 years ago. Today, China is the largest producer of fava beans.

GARDEN PEAS are seeds found in an elongated green pod. The pods grow on a climbing vine known as *Pisum sativum*, which is found in all temperate zones. Peas are among the top ten vegetable crops grown in the world. They were first used by the Chinese in 2000 BCE. Peas are mentioned in the Bible and for many years were used in the dry form only.

GARLIC is the bulb of the plant *Allium sativum*. It has a strong, distinctive flavor and odor. Garlic consists of separate cloves and is used as a seasoning. It is a perennial herb native to Central Asia.

KALE is the ruffled or crinkled leaf of a variety of cabbage called *Brassica oleracea acephala*. The leaves do not form a tight head. Kale is high in calcium.

KIDNEY BEANS are known as *Phaseolus vulgaris*. They are native to Mexico and Peru and are cultivated for their seeds. They are reddish brown in color.

LEMONS are small, yellow, egg-shaped citrus fruits that grow on a spiny tree. They have an aromatic rind and acidic, juicy pulp. Lemons are native to Southeast Asia. In the United States, lemons are the sixth leading fruit crop. Worldwide, Italy is the largest producer of lemons.

LENTILS are seeds which grow in pods on a leguminous plant known as *Lens esculenta* or *Lens culinaris*. There are two varieties of lentils. Brown lentils were cultivated by the ancient Egyptians and Greeks. Brown lentils grow two per small pod and are greenish brown in color. Red lentils are orange-red in color and cook more quickly because they are split in half when dried. Lentils are a good source of vitamin B6.

MILLET is the white seed of the plant, *Panicum miliaceium*. Globally, eighty-five percent of the millet crop is used for food. Millions of people in India, Africa, China, and parts of the Soviet Union depend on millet for seventy percent or more of their caloric intake. In North America, millet, which is grown on a grass, is used mostly for hay. Ninety-four percent of millet is produced in Asia and Africa. China alone produces forty-seven percent.

MISO is a fermented soybean paste and a popular food throughout East Asia, especially Japan. Miso is made out of soybeans, salt, and a starter. The beans undergo a natural fermentation process aided by microorganisms. Miso is aged in wooden barrels for about three years before reaching the marketplace. The three most popular types of miso in the United States include red, made from rice and soybeans; hatcho, made from soybeans alone; and barley, made from barley and soybeans.

MOLASSES is a thick dark syrup that is produced when sugarcane juice is boiled down and the raw sugar is extracted. Blackstrap molasses results from the third stage of refining white sugar. Blackstrap molasses is high in iron and calcium.

MUSHROOMS are fleshy fungi of the class *Basidiomycetes*. Some mushrooms are edible, while others are poisonous and should not be consumed. There are about 38,000 types of mushrooms worldwide. The most common mushroom found in the United States has a white umbrella-shaped cap borne on a stalk. Mushrooms are a good source of riboflavin.

OATS are seeds that grow on any of several grasses of the genus *Avena*, especially *Avena sativa*. Wild stocks of oats first grew in Asia. Oats rank sixth among cereal grains. Today the Soviet Union is the largest producer of oats.

OKRA is a mucilaginous green pod that grows on the tall tropical and semi-tropical plant known as *Hibiscus esculentus*. Okra is native to Africa and also is known as gumbo.

ONIONS are round edible bulbs composed of tight, concentric layers, which have a pungent odor and taste. The onion plant, *Allium cepa*, is cultivated worldwide as a vegetable. Onions are native to the central part of Asia between Iran and Pakistan and toward southern Russia.

ORANGES are round fruits with a yellowish-red rind and a sectioned pulpy interior. Oranges have a sweet acid juice and are high in vitamin C. Oranges grow on several evergreen trees of the genus *Citrus*, cultivated in tropical and subtropical regions. The trees have fragrant white flowers. There are different types of oranges, including *Citrus aurantium*, Seville or sour orange. There also is *Citrus sinensis*, the sweet orange which is native to the area between South China and Indochina. Twenty-nine percent of oranges worldwide are grown in the United States. Florida is the leading producer.

PAPAYAS are large yellow fruits native to Central America. They grow on the *Carica papaya*, a tropical American evergreen.

PEACHES are single-seeded fruits with a red-tinted, yellow skin and yellow flesh. Peaches are soft and juicy when ripe. Peach classification is based on how difficult it is to remove the pit. The most common varieties are known as freestone and clingstone. Peaches grow on the *Pronus persica* tree. They were eaten in China over 4,000 years ago. The peach found its way to Persia (Iran) and is known there as the Persian Apple. Today, the United States and Italy are the leading producers of peaches.

PEANUTS grow on a vine known as *Arachis hupogaea*, which is native to tropical America and widely cultivated in semi-tropical regions. The tree has yellow flowers. The stalks bend over and the seed pod, which contains the peanuts, grows and ripens underground. The peanut is also called a groundnut. It evolved thousands of years ago in South America. Today eighty percent of all peanuts are produced in Asia and Africa, especially in India.

PEARS are large fruits with round bottoms that taper inward toward the stem. However, some pears are completely round. Pears are covered with a smooth yellow, russet, or red skin when ripe. There are several hundred varieties of pears. Pears are indigenous to western Asia. The Bartlett pear is the most commonly found pear in the United States. Today, Italy is the largest producer of pears. Pears are closely related to the apple and are a good source of fiber. Pears can be eaten fresh, baked, or cooked and can be prepared much the same way that apples are.

PINE NUTS are the seeds of certain pine trees, such as the *pinon*. The seeds are beige in color.

PINEAPPLES are large fleshy fruits native to South America. They grow on a tropical American plant known as *Ananas comosus*, which has large, swordlike leaves. The pineapple is thought to have originated in Brazil. Today China is the leading producer of pineapples.

PINTO BEANS are a form of the common string bean that has mottled seeds. They are grown chiefly in the southwestern United States.

POTATOES are starchy tubers that come from the plant *Solanum tubersosum*, which is native to South America. Potato skins are yellow, brown, or red in color. The potato is also called the Irish potato and the white potato. Potatoes were first cultivated between four and seven thousand years ago in the Andes Mountains of Bolivia and Peru. Potatoes are not related to sweet potatoes or yams.

PRUNES are dried plums. They look like over-sized, dark raisins. Prunes are an excellent source of iron and fiber.

RAISINS are dried sweet grapes of several varieties and are dried either in the sun or artificially. Their name comes from the Latin word *racemus*, meaning cluster of grapes or berries. Raisins have been enjoyed since ancient times. Today, California is the largest producer of raisins.

RICE is the starchy seed of a cereal grass known as *Oryza sativa*, cultivated extensively in warm climates. Rice is a staple food throughout the world. Ninety-four percent is produced in the Orient. Rice provides a majority of the food for over half of humanity.

SCALLIONS are green in color with a tiny white bulb. They are young onions which are harvested before the bulb enlarges.

SEITAN is wheat gluten that has been cooked in soy sauce. It is commonly eaten in China, Korea, Russia, and the Middle East. To make seitan, water is added to wheat flour. The mixture is kneaded to a consistency similar to that of bread dough. The bran and starch then are rinsed repeatedly out of the dough until only the gluten remains. The gluten then is simmered in a broth. Oriental stores carry wheat gluten. They call it mien ching or yu mien ching. The broth seitan is simmered in is high in sodium.

SPINACH is the succulent green leaf of the widely cultivated plant *Spinacia oleracea*. It is native to Asia. Today, the United States, the Netherlands, and Scandinavia are the major producers of spinach.

SQUASH is a fleshy fruit with a hard rind which grows on any of a variety of plants of the genus *Cucurbita*. Its wild ancestors are native to the area between Mexico and Guatemala. Today, China is the largest producer of squash. There are many popular varities of squash available in the United States. Summer squashes such as yellow squash and zucchini are soft and watery. Winter squashes such as acorn squash, butternut squash, and vegetable spaghetti, are mature, hard skinned, and have a mildly flavored, finely-grained flesh.

STRAWBERRIES are the world's leading berry-type fruit. The strawberry is a small, red fruit that is an excellent source of vitamin C. When ripe, it is extremely sweet. Strawberry seeds grow on the outside of the fruit; thus, in a botanical sense, they are really not berries. Today, the United States is the largest producer of strawberries.

STRING BEANS are narrow green pods also known as green beans or snap beans. If the pod is yellow it is known as a wax bean. These beans grow on the climbing plant called *Phaseolus vulgaris*.

TEMPEH (pronounced tem-pay) is a staple in Indonesia produced by fermenting pre-soaked and cooked soybeans and sometimes a grain with a culture called rhizopus. The soybeans are hulled before being cooked and inoculated with a starter culture grown on hibiscus leaves. The fermentation process binds the beans together and gives them flavor. Tempeh is an excellent source of protein. If gray or black spots appear on the tempeh, it is the result of natural sporulation and not indicative of spoilage. Tempeh can be fried in a little oil, steamed, boiled, or baked. It is often mixed with grains and vegetables in casseroles.

TOFU, also known as bean curd and soy cheese, is made from soy milk in a similar fashion to the way cheese is made from milk. The soy milk is heated until it boils, a curdling agent is added, and then the curds are separated from the whey. The curds are pressed together to form blocks of tofu. Tofu can be bought in several forms including soft, which is great for dips and dressings, and firm, which is good for stews, etc. Tofu was made originally in China, where it is called dou-fu, from a variety of beans and peas. In fact, tofu is still made from mung beans in some places. Tofu has grown in popularity in the United States and can be found in many supermarkets.

TOMATOES are fruits that are usually red in color, although yellow and orange varieties do exist. They grow on the plant *Lycoperscion esculentum* which is native to South America. Contemporary tomatoes derive from their primitive ancestor, the cherry tomato, which first grew in the Peru-Ecuador area. Today the United States is the largest producer of this vitamin C-rich fruit.

UNBLEACHED WHITE FLOUR is a variety of flour that has had most of the bran and germ removed and is not a whole grain. However, it has not been bleached with chlorides and is often grown organically. Unbleached white flour is not as nutritious as whole wheat flour, but is better than bleached flour.

WATER CHESTNUTS are corms, underwater stem tips, from which a kind of water grass sprouts. Water chestnuts have a sweet crispness like coconut and are off-white in color. They are popular in Oriental cooking and are called ma tai in the Cantonese dialect of Chinese.

WHOLE WHEAT PASTRY FLOUR is made from soft winter wheat and is lower in gluten than flour derived from hard wheat. Whole wheat pastry flour is used to make baked goods that are tender and finely textured. It often is not stoneground, but rather milled in a hammer mill that reduces the soft white or soft red wheat to small particles. Whole wheat pastry flour is not as coarse in texture as whole wheat flour.

ZUCCHINI is a variety of squash that is elongated and has a smooth, thin, dark green rind.

HERBS AND SPICES

ALLSPICE tastes like a combination of cloves, cinnamon, and nutmeg. It comes from the purple, pear-size fruit of the tree, *Pimenta officinalis*. Most allspice is produced in Jamaica.

CARAWAY SEEDS are pungent aromatic seeds of the *Carum carvi* plant. This plant has finely divided leaves and clusters of small white flowers. Caraway seeds are used in baking and cooking. Most of the caraway seeds found in the United States are imported from the Netherlands.

CAYENNE PEPPER is a condiment made from the pungent fruit of a variety of the plant known as *Capsicum frutescens*. It is also called cayenne or red pepper. Cayenne pepper is made by grinding dried chili peppers. The chili peppers are native to the area around the Cayenne River in French Guiana. Cayenne pepper should be used sparingly because it is a very hot spice.

CHILI is the pungent fruit of several varieties of a woody plant known as *Capsicum frutescens*. The powdered form is made by grinding the fruit after it has been dried. Chili powder is very high in vitamin A.

CINNAMON is the yellowish-brown bark of one of two trees, *Cinnamomum zeylanicum* or *Cinnamomum lourer*. The bark is dried, and often ground. Cinnamon is native to Ceylon (Sri Lanka), India, and Malaysia.

CORIANDER is the dried fruit of the small annual plant,*Coriandrum sativum*, which is native to the Mediterranean region. It is usually imported from Morocco.

CUMIN is the aromatic seed of an Old World plant known as *Cuminum cyminum*. The plant has finely divided leaves and small white pinkish flowers. Often, the seeds are ground into a powdered form. Cumin has been used as a spice since Biblical times.

CURRY is a blend of spices that originated in India and is used often in Indian dishes, including sauces and relishes.

DILL is the leaf or seed of an aromatic herb known as *Anethum graveolens*. The plant has finely dissected leaves and small yellow flowers. It is native to southwestern Asia.

GINGER is the pungent, aromatic, rootstock of the plant *Zingiber officinale*, found in tropical Asia. It has yellowish-green flowers. It often is dried and powdered to be used as a flavoring or as a sweetmeat in a sugared form. Ginger often is used in Chinese cooking.

MARJORAM is the leaf of an aromatic plant known as *Majorana hortensis*. The plant has small purplish-white flowers. Marjoram is also called sweet marjoram. It is native to West Asia and the Mediterranean region. Marjoram is a perennial herb belonging to the mint family.

MINT originated in the Old World and grows on various plants of the genus *Mentha*, characteristically having aromatic foliage and flowers. There are about 3,200 different types of mint.

MUSTARD is a tiny yellowish-brown, round seed that often is ground into a powder or paste. It grows on any of various plants of the genus *Brassica*, native to Europe and Asia. The plant has four-petaled, yellow flowers and slender pods.

NUTMEG is derived from the hard aromatic seeds of the evergreen tree known as *Myristica fragrans*, native to the East Indies and cultivated elsewhere in the tropics. Nutmeg is used as a spice when grated or ground.

OREGANO is an herb made from the dried leaves of a species of marjoram known as *Origanum vulgare*. It is popular in Italian cuisine.

PAPRIKA is a mild, powdered seasoning made from the dried pods of sweet red peppers. Paprika is dark, vivid, reddish-orange in color. It is the national spice of Hungary and used extensively in Spanish cooking.

PARSLEY is the dried, curled leaf of the cultivated herb *Petroselinum*. Parsley is used both as a seasoning and as a garnish. It originated in the Mediterranean area and is an excellent source of vitamins A and C. Parsley is also rich in iron.

PEPPER is the dried, berrylike, blackish fruit of the plant *Piper nigrum*, which is a woody vine of the East Indies. Pepper is a pungent spice. It is called black pepper when the whole berry is ground and white pepper when the shell has been removed before grinding.

SESAME SEEDS come from the plant *Sesamum indicum*, which is grown mostly in India, as well as China and Sudan. Sesame seeds are beige in color and are sometimes ground to form sesame butter or tahini.

SWEET BASIL is the herb, *Ocimum basilicum*, which is native to the Old World. It consists of spikes of small white flowers and aromatic leaves, which are used as seasoning. Sweet basil originally came from India and Iran.

TARRAGON is the leaf of the herb known as *Artemisia dracunculus*, which is native to Europe and Asia. It is used both in its fresh and dried form. Tarragon originated in Siberia. There are two varieties. One is Russian and the other is French. In the United States, the French variety is used most often.

THYME is the leaf of several aromatic herbs or low shrubs of the genus *Thymus*, especially *Thymus vulgaris*, which is found in southern Europe near the mountains along the Riviera. The plant has small purplish flowers and the leaves are used as seasoning.

TURMERIC is the powdered rootstock from the *Curcuma longa* plant of India. It is used as a condiment and as a yellow dye. Turmeric is native to southeastern Asia and is in the same family as ginger. Turmeric is used to give mustard its yellow color.

VEGAN NUTRITION

INTRODUCTION

Eating is one of the most basic acts we perform and it is something the majority of people don't even think about! Many factors influence the foods we select -- cost, availability, taste, appearance, religious or ethical principles, and so forth. Nutrition also influences food choices. For example, you may select whole-wheat bread over white bread; fresh fruit over sweetened, canned fruit; and a baked potato over French fries.

Can a vegan diet, chosen for health, environmental, ethical, or other reasons meet nutritional needs? Absolutely! The key to a nutritionally sound vegan diet is variety. Just as you would worry about a friend who only ate hamburgers, you should also worry about a friend who only eats potato chips and salad. A healthy and varied vegan diet includes fruits, vegetables, plenty of leafy greens, whole grain products, nuts, seeds, and legumes. It's that easy.

In fact, if you stopped reading right now and went out and ate a wide variety of foods, chances are good that you would have a nutritionally adequate diet. A vegan diet requires no more careful planning than does a meat-centered diet. And, in fact, since meat-eaters are more likely than are vegetarians to die of diet-related diseases like heart attacks, certain cancers, and hypertension, perhaps meat-eating Americans should spend more time properly planning their diets.

We are writing this section on vegan nutrition to explain how a vegan diet can meet nutritional needs. You may use the facts which we present for reassurance, to improve your diet, or to share with others.

To simplify matters, the discussion of each nutrient will feature a summary paragraph, in bold type, which can be used to provide a quick idea of the most important facts about that nutrient. The end of this section features a glossary of nutrition-related terms and a list of books for further reading.

NUTRITION IS A SCIENCE

Summary: Epidemiological, clinical, and animal studies are all used in nutrition research. Most scientists believe each type of study has its strengths and limitations. Studies are the basis of nutritional recommendations so recommendations change as knowledge about nutritional requirements is acquired.

Nutrition is a science, just as chemistry, biology, and physics are sciences. Since nutrition is a science, it involves research and the use of scientific methods to answer questions. The questions which nutrition scientists ask are often about which foods and how much of those foods people should eat. Scientists design research studies to answer specific questions. Studies may differ in their design and in the method they use to answer a question.

For example, to answer the question "What can I eat to keep from getting cancer?", one scientist might collect information on the diets of groups of people with high rates of cancer and those of people with low rates of cancer. The scientist would then compare the diets of these two groups. Another scientist might feed a group of people a food to see if it would improve the function of their immune system. A third scientist might use rats to see which foods protect them when they are exposed to something known to cause cancer.

These types of studies are examples of epidemiological, clinical, and animal studies, respectively. Most scientists see advantages and disadvantages with each type of study.

Epidemiology is the study of populations. Often in epidemiological studies, people are asked to describe their diet, either current or past. The amounts of different substances in their diets are then correlated with incidence of certain diseases or conditions. Epidemiological studies may also measure the levels of substances such as vitamins or minerals in blood or urine and attempt to correlate these levels with diet or health.

The major strength of epidemiological studies is that they are able to look at large groups of people. Often people from more than one region or more than one country are included in an epidemiological study. The size of this kind of study can give information about a variety of ages as well as the effect of gender or ethnic origin. Epidemiological studies look at people, so the results of these studies are directly applicable to humans and do not have to be extrapolated from animals.

On the other hand, there are limitations to epidemiological studies, particularly those which are based on people's descriptions of what they eat. There are several different tools available to collect this information, but all have some limitations. They all rely on the subject to accurately describe what they eat. This is difficult for many people. If you were a subject in a nutrition study, and you were asked to tell an investigator everything that you ate or drank yesterday, would you remember everything? Would you know how much of each food you had eaten? And how representative of your "typical" diet would that one day's intake be? Besides the limitations due to inaccurate reporting of subjects, another limitation is that investigators are unable to know all the factors affecting their subjects. For example, subjects may have a high rate of cancer because of exposure to radiation, not due to dietary factors at all.

Clinical studies also use human subjects, but these studies are often smaller than epidemiological studies. They modify people's diets or activity levels and then study the effects of these changes.

As with epidemiological studies, an advantage of clinical studies is that they use human subjects so the results of these studies are directly applicable to humans. An additional strength of clinical studies is that they are more controlled. Often in a clinical study, subjects are housed in a metabolic unit, where all food is provided and activity is closely monitored. This allows investigators to know exactly what is going on with their subjects.

A draw-back of this type of study is that very few people live in a controlled setting so the results of these studies may not be the same as those of real life. Also, people are unwilling to live in a metabolic ward for a long time. If a scientist is trying to answer a question about something that takes many years to occur, the results of a clinical study may not be helpful.

Animal studies are used because they allow investigators to have more control than is possible in human studies. Often laboratory animals are bred for research so that the scientist knows their genetic history. Laboratory animals are often maintained on monotonous regimens and tests are performed on them which would not be permitted on humans. Often, animal studies are inexpensive, compared to human studies.

Many people see moral reasons not to experiment on animals. However, ethical issues aside, the major concern with doing animal studies is the question of whether or not results of animal studies are applicable to humans. Although animals and humans are similar in many ways, there are also some major differences. For example, vitamin C is an essential nutrient for humans but not for rats or rabbits. Some of these differences between animals and humans are known so that certain species are not used for certain experiments. For example, vitamin C studies would not usually be done in rats or rabbits. In other cases, differences between the response of animals and that of humans is not known or is controversial. Assuming that humans would respond the same way that animals do, in these cases, could lead to false recommendations.

Advantages and limitations of tissue and cell culture studies are similar to those of animal studies.

Often we are faced with newspaper headlines like "Coffee Drinking Leads to Pancreatic Cancer" or "Vegans have a Deficiency of Vitamin X". These are frequently based on the result of one study. When you read a report like this or hear the latest nutrition news on radio or television, consider the strengths and limitations of each type of nutrition study. Usually one study is not enough to answer a large question in an area as complex as nutrition.

Normally, when a controversial study is published, other scientists begin to do experiments to see if they can get similar results. If several scientists, using different methods, come to similar conclusions, more faith can be placed in their results.

Often the results of a variety of studies are used to make nutritional recommendations. Recommendations made by groups such as the National Academy of Sciences, The American Dietetic Association, the American Cancer Society, and the American Heart Association are usually made by a committee of scientists who have conducted a thorough review of the existing information on the subject. Recommendations change due to new information and to new ways of looking at previously collected information.

We do know a lot about nutrition and our knowledge base is growing daily. Nutrition studies can be used to make recommendations about what people should eat to achieve good health. In this nutrition section, the results of scientific studies will be used to make recommendations specifically aimed at people following vegan diets.

RECOMMENDATIONS FOR VEGANS

Summary: A vegan diet conforms to recommendations made to reduce the risk of the major chronic diseases such as heart disease and cancer. The long-term quality of an individual's diet should be used to assess its nutritional adequacy. The Recommended Dietary Allowances (RDAs) are commonly used to make recommendations for nutrient intake.

What do the various government agencies that make recommendations about the nation's health have to say about vegan diets? Very little is explicitly stated. However, careful reading between the lines evokes the idea that diets similar to those followed by many American vegans are being recommended by governmental and scientific groups.

In 1988, then Surgeon General C. Everett Koop submitted the first Report on Nutrition and Health (1). In Dr. Koop's opening message he states, "...overconsumption of certain dietary components is now a major concern for Americans. While many food factors are involved, chief among them is the disproportionate consumption of foods high in fats, often at the expense of foods high in complex carbohydrates and fiber -- such as vegetables, fruits, and whole grain products -- that may be more conducive to health" (1). It certainly sounds as if those foods which predominate in a vegan diet are being endorsed by the former Surgeon General. This report goes on to recommend a single type of diet for all Americans which will reduce the risk of the major chronic diseases (coronary heart disease, hypertension, cancer, diabetes, and obesity). The recommended diet is low in fat, saturated fat, cholesterol, and sodium, and high in complex carbohydrates and fiber -- a vegan diet?

Vegan diets, which emphasize grains, legumes, vegetables, and fruits and avoid foods of animal origin, are generally low in fat, low in saturated fat, high in complex carbohydrates and fiber, and absolutely free of cholesterol. Cholesterol is only found in foods of animal origin. The sodium content of vegan diets varies depending on the amount of processed or canned foods eaten and the amount of salt added in cooking or at the table.

Recommendations similar to those of the Surgeon General, were made by the Committee on Diet and Health of the National Academy of Sciences (2). Their recommendations are more specific: 30% or less of calories from fat, less than 10% of calories from saturated fat, less than 300 mg per day of cholesterol, more than 55% of calories from carbohydrate, and a moderate intake of protein. The dietary recommendations of the American Heart Association (3,4), the National Cholesterol Education Program (5), and the National Cancer Institute (6) are all consistent with a vegan diet. The American Dietetic Association states that "scientific data suggests a positive relationship between vegetarian diets and risk reduction for several chronic diseases" (7).

Recommended Dietary Allowances

About every five years, a committee of nutritional scientists is selected by the National Academy of Sciences (a private non-profit group which advises the government on science and health issues). This committee is instructed to review all available information and develop recommendations for the amounts of essential nutrients needed by Americans. Since nutrition is a rapidly changing field, recommendations do change. This committee produces the Recommended Dietary Allowances which are commonly called the RDAs.

The RDAs are defined as "the levels of intake of essential nutrients that, on the basis of scientific knowledge, are judged by the Food and Nutrition Board to be adequate to meet the known nutrient needs of practically all healthy persons" (8). They are developed to contain a margin of safety to insure that they meet the needs of practically all healthy people. Since there is a margin of safety, if your diet does not meet the RDA for every nutrient, every day, you should not be concerned. It is more important to consider the quality of your diet over time.

Generally, when making recommendations for the amounts of nutrients needed for vegans, we will refer to the RDAs. In some instances, we will turn to the recommendations of international bodies such as the World Health Organization (WHO) for a different perspective.

References

1. Department of Health and Human Services: *The Surgeon's General's Report on Nutrition and Health.* Washington, DC: Government Printing Office, 1988.

2. Committee on Diet and Health, Food and Nutrition Board: *Diet and Health. Implications for Reducing Chronic Disease.* Washington, DC: National Academy Press, 1989.

3. American Heart Association Nutrition Committee: Coronary risk factor statement for the American public. *Circulation* 72: 1135A, 1985.

4. American Heart Association Nutrition Committee: Dietary guidelines for healthy American adults. *Circulation* 77: 721A, 1989.

5. National Cholesterol Education Program Expert Panel: Report of the National Cholesterol Education Program Expert Panel on detection, evaluation, and treatment of high blood cholesterol in adults. *Arch Intern Med* 148: 36-69, 1988.

6. Butrum RR, Clifford CK, Lanza E: NCI dietary guidelines: Rationale. *Am J Clin Nutr* 48: 888-895, 1988.

7. Position of The American Dietetic Association: Vegetarian diets. *J Am Diet Assoc* 88: 351-355, 1988.

8. Food and Nutrition Board, National Research Council: *Recommended Dietary Allowances,* 10th ed. Washington, DC: National Academy Press, 1989.

CALORIES, WEIGHT GAIN, AND WEIGHT LOSS

Summary: Protein, fat, and carbohydrate all provide energy in the form of calories. Fat is a more concentrated source of calories. To lose weight, eat less and exercise more. To gain weight, eat more.

In a discussion of nutrition, the words "calories" and "energy" are interchangeable. That's because a calorie is a measure of the amount of energy provided by a food. Adequate energy is essential. We need enough calories (that is, energy) to function every day. If enough food (calories) is not eaten, the body will break down both muscle protein and fat, wounds will not heal, children will not grow, and individuals of any age will eventually become ill and die.

There is an easy way to see whether or not your diet contains enough calories. Look at your weight. Normally, non-pregnant adults should be neither losing nor gaining weight. Caloric intake should equal energy output. In other words, the calories (energy) from foods you eat should be approximately the same as the calories you "burn up" in activity. If you are losing weight unintentionally, you are probably not taking in enough calories. Similarly, if you are gaining weight, you are taking in more calories than you expend.

Food provides energy in the form of carbohydrates, protein, and fat. Each gram of fat in a food provides 9 calories, as compared with 4 calories for each gram of carbohydrate or protein. In addition to a gram of fat having more than twice the number of calories of a gram of protein or carbohydrate, we seem to be more efficient at storing calories from fat (1).

Elliot Danforth, Jr. and coworkers at the University of Vermont (1), overfed volunteers a mixed diet of carbohydrate and fat. Volunteers gained little weight even though they took in more calories than they expended. A similar group of subjects had their excess calories supplied as fat. They gained a lot of weight.

This suggests that those trying to lose weight should reduce dietary fat intake. In fact, decreasing dietary fat may be more important than decreasing calorie intake for dieters.

Vegans as a group tend to be lean. In other words, a vegan has a better chance of not being overweight than a non-vegetarian (2). This may be because most foods vegans eat are low in fat. Foods which are high fat, such as oils, nuts, seeds, avocados, tofu, and olives, are often used in limited amounts. Thus, vegan diets are usually lower in fat than typical American diets and often lower in calories. The kinds of foods eaten are frequently higher in bulk which can limit the amount of food eaten.

Obesity is a significant risk factor for many chronic diseases including coronary heart disease, high blood pressure, diabetes, and some kinds of cancer. The National Health and Nutrition Examination Survey (NHANES II), a comprehensive survey of many thousands of people in the United States, found that almost 25% of adults were overweight (3). While the causes of obesity vary widely, certainly the adoption of a vegan diet should reduce the risk of obesity.

Whereas bulky foods, as are commonly eaten on vegan diets, are not a problem for many people, they can make it difficult for some young children or pregnant women to gain weight. Individuals in these groups can become full before getting the calories they need. For those who need to increase weight, grow, or stop losing weight, it is sometimes necessary to increase the fat and thereby increase the number of calories in the diet. Since fat is a more concentrated source of calories than either carbohydrate or protein, moderate use of higher fat foods such as nuts, seeds, avocados, nut butters (e.g. peanut butter, almond butter), and seed butters (e.g. tahini which is also called sesame butter) can help with weight gain. Vegans, especially children and others trying to gain weight, should eat small meals or snacks throughout the day.

References

1. Danforth E, Jr: Diet and obesity. *Am J Clin Nutr* 41: 1132-1145, 1985.

2. Brown BT and Bergan JG: The dietary status of the "new" vegetarians. *J Am Diet Assoc* 67: 455-459, 1979.

3. National Center for Health Statistics: *Anthropometric reference data and prevalence of overweight, United States 1976-1980.* Hyattsville, MD: National Center for Health Statistics, 1987.

PROTEIN

Summary: It is very easy for a vegan diet to meet the recommendations for protein, as long as calorie intake is adequate. Strict protein combining is not necessary; it is more important to eat a varied diet throughout the day.

Some Americans are obsessed with protein. Vegans are bombarded with questions about where they get their protein. Athletes used to eat thick steaks before competition because they thought it would improve their performance. Protein supplements are sold at health food stores. This concern about protein is misplaced. In reality, we need small amounts of protein. Only one calorie out of every ten we take in needs to come from protein (1). Athletic performance is actually improved by a high carbohydrate diet, not a high protein diet (2). Protein supplements are expensive, unnecessary, and even harmful for some people.

In this country, vegan diets are almost never deficient in protein. Vegan diets are often lower in protein than standard American diets (SAD), but with protein, more (than the RDA) is not necessarily better. A high protein diet is not especially health-promoting and may even increase the risk of osteoporosis or kidney disease (3). The RDA for protein for adults is 63 grams per day for men and 50 grams per day for women (1). An upper limit of 70 grams per day of protein has been recommended (4).

It is very easy for a vegan diet to meet the recommendations for protein. Nearly all vegetables, beans, grains, nuts, and seeds contain some, and often much, protein. Fruits, sugars, fats, and alcohol do not provide much protein, so a diet based only on these foods would have a good chance of being too low in protein. However, not many vegans we know live on only bananas, hard candy, margarine, and beer. Vegans eating varied diets containing vegetables, beans, grains, nuts, and seeds rarely have any difficulty getting enough protein as long as their diet contains enough energy (calories) to maintain weight. (See Tables 1 and 2 (pages 141-142) and the sections on Pregnancy, Lactation, and Infants and Children (pages 177-198) for information about protein needs during these special times.)

Table 1: Sample Menus Showing How Easy It Is To Meet Protein Needs

		Protein (grams)
Breakfast:		
	1 cup Oatmeal	4
	1 cup Soymilk	10
	1 Bagel	6
Lunch:		
	2 slices Whole Wheat Bread	5
	2 Tbsp Peanut Butter	8
Dinner:		
	4 oz firm Tofu	20
	1 cup Broccoli	5
	1 cup Brown Rice	5
TOTAL		63 grams
Male Protein RDA:		63 grams

Breakfast:		
	2 slices Whole Wheat Toast	5
	1 Tbsp Peanut Butter	4
Lunch:		
	1 cup Soy Yogurt	10
	2 Tbsp Almonds	2.8
	1 Baked Potato	4.5
Dinner:		
	1 cup Lentils	18
	1 cup Bulgur	6
TOTAL		50.3 grams
Female Protein RDA:		50 grams

Additional foods should be added to these menus to provide adequate calories and to meet additional nutritional requirements.

Table 2 shows the amount of protein in various vegan foods and also the number of grams of protein per 100 calories. To meet protein recommendations, the typical adult male needs only 2.2 grams of protein per 100 calories and the typical adult female needs only 2.3 grams of protein per 100 calories. These recommendations can be easily met from vegan sources.

Table 2: Protein Content of Selected Vegan Foods

FOOD	AMOUNT	PROTEIN (gm)	PROTEIN (gm/100 cal)
Tempeh	1 cup	31	9.4
Soybeans, cooked	1 cup	29	9.7
Seitan	4 ounces	21	15.4
Tofu, firm	4 ounces	20	10.9
Lentils, cooked	1 cup	18	7.8
Kidney beans, cooked	1 cup	15	6.0
Lima beans, cooked	1 cup	15	6.9
Chickpeas, cooked	1 cup	15	5.6
Black beans, cooked	1 cup	15	6.6
Pinto beans, cooked	1 cup	14	6.0
Black-eyed peas, cooked	1 cup	13	6.6
Vegetarian baked beans	1 cup	12	5.1
Quinoa, cooked	1 cup	11	4.7

FOOD	AMOUNT	PROTEIN (gm)	PROTEIN (gm/100 cal)
Soy yogurt	1 cup	10	11.1
Soy milk, commercial, plain	1 cup	10	6.5
Tofu, regular	4 ounces	10	10.6
Peanut butter	2 TB	8	4.3
Sunflower seeds	1/4 cup	8	3.3
Peas, cooked	1 cup	8	6.4
Bulgur, cooked	1 cup	6	3.9
Bagel	1 medium	6	3.7
Almonds	1/4 cup	5.5	2.7
Spinach, cooked	1 cup	5	12.2
Broccoli, cooked	1 cup	5	11.4
Cashews	1/4 cup	5	2.5
Brown rice, cooked	1 cup	5	2.4
Almond butter	2 TB	5	2.5
Whole wheat bread	2 slices	5	4.5
Potato	1 medium	4.5	2.0
Hazelnuts	1/4 cup	4.5	2.1

Source: Composition of Foods, USDA Handbook 8.

The RDA for protein for adult males is 63 grams per day; for adult females it is 50 grams per day.

Table 3 (page 145) shows the amount of protein in selected foods from animal sources. Many of these foods are high in protein, so high that it may be difficult to remain below the suggested upper limit for protein which is 4.5 grams of protein per 100 calories for adults (5). A varied vegan diet can provide adequate, but not excessive protein.

What about combining or complementing protein? Doesn't that make the protein issue much more complex? Let's look at a little background on the myth of complementing proteins. Protein is made up of amino acids, often described as building blocks of protein. We actually have a biological requirement for amino acids, not for protein. Humans cannot make nine of the twenty common amino acids, so these amino acids are considered to be essential. In other words, we must get these amino acids from our diets. We need all nine of these amino acids for our body to make protein.

Eggs, cow's milk, meat, and fish have been designated as high quality protein (1). This means that they have large amounts of all the essential amino acids. Soybeans, quinoa (a grain), and spinach also are considered high quality protein. Other protein sources of non-animal origin usually have all of the essential amino acids, but the amounts of one or two of these amino acids may be low. For example, grains are lower in lysine (an essential amino acid) and legumes are lower in methionine (another essential amino acid) than those protein sources designated as high quality protein.

Frances Moore Lappe, in her book *Diet for a Small Planet* (6) advocated the combining of a food low in one amino acid with another food containing large amounts of that amino acid. This got to be a very complicated process, with each meal having specific amounts of certain foods in order to be certain of getting a favorable amino acid mix. Many people got discouraged with the complexity of this approach. Actually, Lappe was being overly conservative to avoid criticism from the "Nutrition Establishment". She has since repudiated strict protein combining, saying "In combatting the myth that meat is the only way to get high quality protein, I reinforced another myth. I gave the impression that in order to get enough protein without meat, considerable care was needed in choosing foods. Actually it is much easier than I thought" (7).

Table 3: Protein Content of Selected Animal-Derived Foods

FOOD	AMOUNT	PROTEIN (gm)	PROTEIN (gm/100 cal)
Sirloin steak	3 oz	26	15.8
Chicken, baked	3 oz	25	15.0
Pork roast	3 oz	23	11.6
Flounder, baked	3 oz	20	20.2
Ground beef	3 oz	20	8.1
Cow's milk	1 cup	8	5.3
Cheddar cheese	1 oz	7	6.1
Egg	1	6	8.0

Source: *Composition of Foods, USDA Handbook 8.*

The RDA for protein for adult males is 63 grams per day; for adult females it is 50 grams per day. An average of no more than 4.5 grams of protein per 100 calories (5) or a total of 70 grams of protein per day is recommended (4).

A 3-ounce portion of meat or fish is a small portion, about the size of the palm of an adult woman's hand.

We recommend eating a variety of unrefined grains, legumes, seeds, nuts, and vegetables throughout the day, so that if one food is low in a particular essential amino acid, another food will make up this deficit (3, 8).

Even if you ate only one food and not the variety of foods typical of a vegan diet, you would probably get enough protein and essential amino acids (9). Remember, almost all protein sources of non-animal origin contain all of the essential amino acids. You would have to eat a lot of the protein source (if there was only one source of protein in your diet) to meet essential amino acid needs. Table 4 (page 147) shows the amounts of various foods an adult male would have to eat if he relied on a single food source for his protein needs. Females would need about 20 percent less of each food due to the lower protein recommendation for women.

References

1. Food and Nutrition Board, National Research Council: *Recommended Dietary Allowances,* 10th ed. Washington, DC: National Academy Press, 1989.

2. Bergstrom J, Hermansen L, Hultman E, Saltin B: Diet, muscle glycogen and physical performance. *Acta Physiol Scan* 71: 140-150, 1967.

3. Position of The American Dietetic Association: Vegetarian diets. *J Am Diet Assoc* 88: 351-355, 1988.

4. Kerstetter JE and Allen LH: Dietary protein increases urinary calcium. *J Nutr* 120: 134-136, 1990.

5. Committee on Diet and Health, Food and Nutrition Board: *Diet and Health. Implications for Reducing Chronic Disease.* Washington, DC: National Academy Press, 1989.

6. Lappe FM: *Diet for a Small Planet.* New York: Ballantine Books, 1971.

7. Lappe FM: *Diet for a Small Planet,* 10th anniversary edition. New York: Ballantine Books, 1982.

8. Harper AE: McCollum and directions in the evaluation of protein quality. *J Agric Food Chem* 29: 429-435, 1981.

9. Kies C: Bioavailability: A factor in protein quality. *J Agric Food Chem* 29: 435-440, 1981.

Table 4: Amounts of Foods Providing Recommended Amounts of Essential Amino Acids

8 cups of cooked corn OR 8 medium potatoes OR 1.1 pounds of tofu OR 6 cups of cooked brown rice

Any one of the above foods, eaten in the amount specified, would provide the recommended amounts of all essential amino acids for an adult male. Females would need about 20% less of each food due to lower recommendations. This concept is illustrated below:

Food	Try	Thr	Iso	Leu	Lys	Met+Cys	Phe+Tyr	Val
8 cups corn	304	1744	1744	4704	1856	1264	3680	2512
8 potatoes	584	1360	1504	2232	2264	1056	3024	2104
1.1 lbs tofu	642	1685	2042	3133	2715	1096	7766	2081
6 cups rice	384	1104	1278	2496	1152	1044	2694	1770
Adult RDA, 174 lb male	**296**	**553**	**790**	**1106**	**948**	**1027**	**1106**	**790**

Source: *Composition of Foods, USDA Handbook 8.*

Amounts of amino acids are in milligrams. Try=tryptophan, Thr=threonine, Iso=isoleucine, Leu=leucine, Lys=lysine, Met+Cys=methionine+cysteine, Phe+Tyr=phenylalanine+tyrosine, Val=valine

FAT

Summary: Vegan diets are free of cholesterol and are generally low in fat. High-fat foods which should be used sparingly include oils, margarine, nuts, nut butters, seed butters, avocado, tofu, and coconut.

Surveys have shown that the American diet gets 37% or more of its calories from fat. Current recommendations are consistent in emphasizing that dietary fat be reduced to 30% or less of total calories to reduce risk of heart disease and certain cancers. Table 5 (page 149) shows what amount of fat would be included in diets of various calorie levels with 10, 20, or 30% fat. For example, a 30% fat diet means that if you eat 2000 calories in a day, 30% or less of those calories (2000 calories x 30% = 600 calories) should come from fat. Since fat has 9 calories per gram, this means no more than 66 grams of fat per day. Table 6 (page 150) provides examples of foods providing 66 grams of fat. We actually need only 2-3% of calories as fat to insure that we get enough of those fatty acids which our bodies need, but cannot produce.

Diets with as little as 10% fat have been successfully used in patients with heart disease (1). Dean Ornish, M.D. and coworkers placed patients with coronary artery disease on one of two regimens. They were either placed on a nearly vegan diet with only 10% of calories from fat, no smoking, stress management, and moderate exercise; or permitted to continue their usual lifestyle. Significant improvements in symptoms such as angina and reductions in arterial blockage were seen in the group on the near-vegan diet. This suggests that a diet which is quite low in fat can be beneficial, even for people who already have heart disease.

Generally vegan diets are low in fat because of their emphasis on grains, legumes, fruits, and vegetables, and their avoidance of meat, eggs, and dairy products which often contain large amounts of fat. Some foods vegans eat such as oils, margarine, nuts, nut butters, tofu, tahini, avocado, and coconut are high in fat. These foods should not be the center of one's diet, but should be used sparingly, more as a condiment than a main course. For example, tofu, by itself, is high in fat. If you ate 300 calories of tofu, 50% of them would be from fat. However, if you steamed tofu and served it over rice with vegetables, a 300 calorie serving of this dish might only have 20% or fewer calories from fat because a smaller amount of tofu was used. In the same way, if you ate an entire bowl of guacamole, it would be very high in fat. If you had a slice of avocado on a sandwich, you would not be eating that much fat.

Table 5. Suggested Daily Fat Intake on Different Calorie Levels

1200 calories:

10% fat	13 grams of fat
20% fat	27 grams of fat
30% fat	40 grams of fat

1500 calories:

10% fat	17 grams of fat
20% fat	33 grams of fat
30% fat	50 grams of fat

1800 calories

10% fat	20 grams of fat
20% fat	40 grams of fat
30% fat	60 grams of fat

2000 calories

10% fat	22 grams of fat
20% fat	44 grams of fat
30% fat	66 grams of fat

2500 calories

10% fat	27 grams of fat
20% fat	55 grams of fat
30% fat	83 grams of fat

Numerous groups have recommended that Americans get 30% or fewer calories from fat; 20% or fewer calories are beginning to be recommended. Diets with as few as 10% of calories from fat have been used in a supervised setting for persons with heart disease.

Diets containing less than 30% of calories as fat are not normally recommended for young children.

Table 6 can be used to help in making food choices. For example, if you normally eat 2000 calories and want a 30% fat diet, you could choose to eat 1 cup of shelled peanuts at one time. Then the rest of the day, you would eat foods with little or no fat. Another choice might be to eat a variety of foods with and without fat throughout the day.

Table 6. Amounts of Foods Providing 600 Calories From Fat

2 Avocados

7 cups of French Fries

3 pounds of Tofu

0.9 cups of shelled Almonds

0.5 cups of Peanut Butter

7 tablespoons of Almond Butter

5 tablespoons of Oil

133 Olives

1.3 cups of Coconut

6 tablespoons of Margarine

1.1 cups of shelled Cashews

1 cup of shelled Peanuts

0.9 cup of shelled Sunflower Seeds

11.5 cups of Potato Chips

Even if one food gets more than 30% of its calories from fat, it may still have a place in a low-fat diet. For example, we include a recipe for cabbage salad which gets 79% of its calories from fat. However, this salad has 9 grams of fat and so is only moderately high in fat. Table 7 shows several combinations of foods which provide 30% of calories as fat.

Table 7. Combinations of Foods Providing 30% of Calories as Fat

1/4 Avocado + 4 slices of Bread

1 cup French Fries + 1 Apple

4 ounces of Tofu + 1/3 cup cooked Rice

1 tablespoon Margarine + 1 medium Potato

1 1/2 tablespoons Tahini + 3/4 cup Chickpeas

Many recipes can be altered so as to reduce their fat content even further. For example, you can saute in water instead of oil or decrease the amount of oil in a recipe. Experiment to see what works for you.

Diets which are very limited in fat (less than 30% of total calories) are not normally recommended for young children. Children need enough calories to grow and fat represents a concentrated source of those calories.

Type of Fat

Fats are categorized according to their chemical structure as saturated, monounsaturated, and polyunsaturated fats. Saturated fats, found mainly in animal fats and in coconut oil, palm oil, and palm kernel oil, are the kind of fats most likely to cause heart disease. Polyunsaturated fats, which are especially high in safflower oil, sunflower oil, soybean oil, and corn oil have long been recommended to replace more saturated fats in order to reduce the risk of heart disease. Recently, much attention has been given to oils high in monounsaturated fats such as olive oil, peanut oil, and canola oil. Some research suggests that these oils can also replace more saturated fats and reduce the risk of heart disease.

As a part of food processing, unsaturated oils may be changed to be chemically more like saturated fats. This process is called hydrogenation. Since hydrogenated oils are more like saturated fat, their use should be limited. For example, if you use margarine, select a brand with liquid soybean oil or liquid safflower oil as the first ingredient instead of hydrogenated soybean oil. This kind of margarine will be softer, as hydrogenation makes the margarine more solid.

What kind of oil should you use? The best choice, based on current knowledge, is one high in either polyunsaturated or monounsaturated fat. Table 8 (page 153) gives the percentage of saturated, monounsaturated, and polyunsaturated fat in various oils and margarines. Good choices include safflower oil, sunflower oil, soybean oil, corn oil, peanut oil, olive oil, and canola oil. Whichever one you choose, use it sparingly since 100% of its calories will come from fat.

Some studies suggest that use of large amounts of polyunsaturated fats increases cancer risk, while other studies show no association between type of fat and cancer. For now, we recommend limiting use of all fats because of the association between total fat intake and risk of heart disease and certain cancers.

Cholesterol

Dietary cholesterol is one substance vegans do not have to be concerned with. Cholesterol is found only in foods of animal origin so the vegan diet is free of cholesterol. Some plants do contain phytosterols, which have a structure similar to cholesterol. However, phytosterols do not affect blood cholesterol levels.

Dietary cholesterol is not necessary since our bodies are able to make all of the cholesterol we need. All of the recipes in this book have no cholesterol.

Reference

1. Ornish D, Brown SE, Scherwitz LW, et al: Can lifestyle changes reverse coronary heart disease? The lifestyle heart trial. *Lancet* 336: 129-133, 1990.

Table 8. Typical Fatty Acid Composition of Vegetable Oils and Animal Fats

Oil or Fat	% of Total Fatty Acids		
	Saturated	Monounsaturated	Polyunsaturated
Coconut oil	92	6	2
Palm kernel oil	82	15	2
Butterfat	63	31	3
Cocoa butter	61	34	3
Palm oil	50	40	10
Beef tallow	46	47	4
Lard	42	48	10
Margarine, butter blend	37	42	21
Cottonseed oil	26	20	55
Margarine, stick, soy (hydrogenated)	22	51	27
Margarine, soft, corn (hydrogenated)	18	41	41
Olive oil	17	72	11
Soybean oil	15	24	61
Peanut oil	14	50	32
Corn oil spread	14	43	43
Corn oil	13	28	59
Sunflower oil	12	19	69
Margarine, soft, safflower (hydrogenated)	12	30	58
Safflower oil	9	13	78
Low-erucic acid rapeseed (canola oil)	6	62	32

Sources: Council on Scientific Affairs: Saturated fatty acids in vegetable oils. JAMA 263: 693-695, 1990 and Composition of Foods, USDA Handbook 8. If you use oil, choose from the shaded portion of the chart.

CALCIUM

Summary: Calcium, needed for strong bones, is found in dark green vegetables, tofu processed with calcium sulfate, and many other foods commonly eaten by vegans. High protein diets appear to lead to increased calcium losses. Calcium requirements for those on lower protein, plant-based diets are believed to be below the usual recommendations.

Calcium is a very important mineral in the human body. Our bones contain large amounts of calcium which helps to make them firm and rigid. Calcium is also needed for many other tasks including nerve and muscle function and blood clotting. These other tasks are so important for survival, that, when dietary calcium is too low, calcium will be lost from bone and used for other critical functions. Calcium in the blood is tightly controlled by the body, so calcium status cannot be assessed by measuring blood calcium levels.

Because of heavy promotion by the American dairy industry, the public often believes that cow's milk is the sole source of calcium. However, other excellent sources of calcium exist so that vegans eating varied diets need not be concerned about getting adequate calcium. Table 9 (page 156) shows the amount of calcium in selected foods. When you realize that there is as much calcium in 5 ounces of firm tofu or 3/4 cups of collard greens as there is in one cup of cow's milk, it is easy to see why groups of people who do not drink cow's milk still have strong bones and teeth.

Tofu is commonly recommended as a good source of calcium. Actually, the amount of calcium in tofu depends on the coagulating agent used to precipitate the soy protein in the process of making tofu. Calcium sulfate and nigari (magnesium chloride) are two commonly used agents. The agent used will be listed on the label under ingredients. Tofu which is prepared with calcium sulfate will contain more calcium than tofu made with nigari.

The amount of calcium in tofu varies from brand to brand. To calculate how much calcium is in the tofu you buy, look at the label. Calcium content will be listed as percent of the U.S.RDA (often 10 or 15%). Since the current U.S.RDA for calcium is 1000 milligrams, multiply the percent U.S.RDA by 10 to get the amount of calcium (in milligrams) in one serving. For example, tofu with 10% of the U.S.RDA for calcium would have 100 milligrams of calcium in one serving.

How much calcium do we need? The RDA for adults age 25 and older is 800 milligrams of calcium per day (1). An intake of 1200 milligrams of calcium per day is recommended for those age 11-24. In other countries, calcium recommendations are lower than in the US. For example, British adults are advised to have a calcium intake of 500 milligrams per day (2) and adults in Japan are told to have 600 milligrams of calcium daily (3). Does only science influence these recommendations or are political and economic factors also at work? (Read *Nutrition Action Health Letter* from Center for Science in the Public Interest, *Vegetarian Journal*, *Guide to Healthy Eating* from Physician's Committee for Responsible Medicine, *Nutrition Week* from the Community Nutrition Institute, *Advertising Age*, and National Dairy Council materials for insight into forces shaping recommendations.)

Calcium requirements may be influenced by high protein intakes (4). High protein diets seem to markedly increase the amount of calcium lost from the body every day (5,6). In fact, when young adults had a protein intake of 48 grams per day (slightly lower than the current RDA) they had no net loss of calcium, even though the amount of calcium in their diet was as low as 500 milligrams daily (7). In contrast, when young adults were on a diet high in protein (112 grams -- typical of many Americans), they lost substantial amounts of calcium in their urine, even when calcium intakes were as high as 1400 milligrams per day (7).

Although phosphorus, another mineral found in foods which are high in protein, does reduce the effects of protein on calcium somewhat, calcium status appears to be more affected by the amount of protein in the diet (5, 6). A protein intake above 70 grams per day is not recommended (6). Of course, this level of protein intake is likely to be exceeded on a meat-based diet or a diet high in dairy products. As Table 10 (page 158) shows, by eating 2 servings of meat or fish, an egg, and 2 cups of milk every day, a person would come close to exceeding the 70 gram upper limit for protein without even considering other protein sources such as breads and vegetables.

Table 9: Calcium Content of Selected Vegan Foods

FOOD	AMOUNT	CALCIUM (mg)
Tofu, firm, processed with calcium sulfate*	4 ounces	250-765
Tofu, regular, processed with calcium sulfate*	4 ounces	120-392
Collard greens, cooked	1 cup	357
Rhubarb, cooked	1 cup	348
Spinach, cooked	1 cup	278
Blackstrap molasses	2 TB	274
Turnip greens, cooked	1 cup	249
Tofu, firm, processed with nigari*	4 ounces	80-230
Kale, cooked	1 cup	179
Sesame seeds	2 TB	176
Okra, cooked	1 cup	176
Soybeans, cooked	1 cup	175
Beet greens, cooked	1 cup	165
Bok choy, cooked	1 cup	158
Tempeh	1 cup	154
Mustard greens, cooked	1 cup	150
Figs, dried or fresh	5 medium	135
Tahini	2 TB	128
Tofu, regular, processed with nigari*	4 ounces	80-146
Swiss chard, cooked	1 cup	102
Almonds	1/4 cup	97
Broccoli, cooked	1 cup	94
Almond butter	2 TB	86
Soymilk, commercial, plain	8 ounces	84

*Read the label on your tofu container to see if it is processed with calcium sulfate or nigari.

(Continued on next page)

The RDA for calcium for adults, 25 and older, is 800 milligrams per day; for those 11-24, the RDA is 1200 milligrams of calcium. United States recommendations are more than 50% higher than the British and Japanese.

Note: Oxalic acid which is found in spinach, rhubarb, chard and beet greens is often said to bind with calcium and reduce absorption. In laboratory experiments, calcium does combine with oxalates. However, at normal dietary intakes, oxalates have little practical effect on calcium absorption (1).

Sources: *Composition of Foods. USDA Handbook 8.*
                  Manufacturer's information.

The type of protein may also be important. At least one study shows that soy protein, even at high levels, does not increase calcium excretion the same way that protein from animal sources does (5).

The RDAs for calcium were made for people consuming typical American high protein diets. Many vegan diets are lower in protein than these typical American diets. For those whose protein intake is lower, but adequate, or whose protein is from non-animal sources, calcium intakes below the RDA are probably adequate.

We recommend that two or more servings of good sources of dietary calcium be eaten daily by adults, along with the use of a diet without excessive protein. Teenagers and young adults (age 20-25) should eat 3 or more servings of foods high in calcium. Regular weight-bearing exercise such as walking, running, or aerobic dance is also recommended to promote strong, healthy bones. Table 11 (page 159) shows several menus which contain more than 800 milligrams of calcium.

Table 10: Protein Content of Selected Foods

FOOD	AMOUNT	PROTEIN (gm)
Cow's milk	8 ounces	8
Egg	1	6
Salmon, pink, canned	4 ounces	22
Beef, ground	4 ounces	26
Chicken	4 ounces	19

Adapted from Havala S: Osteoporosis. Beyond a simple answer. Vegetarian Journal 5: 11, 1986.

Table 11: Sample Menus Providing More Than 800 milligrams of Calcium

	Calcium (mg)
Breakfast:	
1 svg Cindy's Light and Fluffy Pancakes (p. 23)	210
Lunch:	
1 svg Hummus on Pita Bread (p. 27)	178
5 Dried Figs	135
Dinner:	
1 svg Scrambled Tofu and Bok Choy over Brown Rice (p. 96)	190
1 svg Green Salad and Tangerine Dressing (p. 39)	30
1 svg Chocolate Pudding (p. 114)	92
TOTAL	835

Breakfast:	
1 svg Tropical Fruit Smoothie (p. 16)	102
1 Toasted Bagel with 2 Tbsp Almond Butter	86
Lunch:	
1 svg Mini Pizzas (p. 34)	235
1 svg Creamed Spinach (p. 68)	121
Dinner:	
1 svg Lemon Rice Soup (p. 46)	82
1 svg Tofu Squash Burgers (p. 102)	135
1 cup Steamed Broccoli	94
TOTAL	855

Additional foods should be added to these menus to provide adequate calories and to meet additional nutritional requirements.

Vegetarian, and especially vegan, diets are often high in fiber due to frequent use of whole grains, beans, fruits, and vegetables. This may be one reason why vegetarians have a lower incidence of heart disease and some kinds of cancer than does the general public. However, one concern with diets high in fiber is that the fiber can bind with minerals, like calcium, in the intestine and thus keep the minerals from being absorbed. Vegan diets may contain 40 or more grams of fiber per day (8). Dietary fiber intakes of 35 grams or less are not believed to have a significant impact on mineral absorption (9). However, humans may be able to adapt to diets with more than 35 grams of dietary fiber, so that, in time, these diets have little effect on calcium absorption. This adaptation apparently occurs in vegans since bone density of vegans appears to be normal (10). If calcium absorption was impaired, bone density of vegans would be expected to be low.

What about osteoporosis? Don't vegans need extra calcium to prevent osteoporosis? In osteoporosis, bones become porous and fragile. The Dairy Council leads us to believe that milk is essential to prevent osteoporosis. In reality, many other foods besides milk (see Table 9, page 156) provide calcium, often without the high dose of protein seen in milk.

Other factors which increase the risk of osteoporosis include small frame size, female sex, aging, heredity, cigarette smoking, excessive alcohol, Caucasian or Oriental race, steroid use, early menopause, and prolonged immobilization.

The most promising way that nutrition can reduce the risk of osteoporosis is by promoting development of a favorable peak bone mass during the first 3 to 4 decades of life. Several studies have shown that vegetarians have the same (11, 12) or larger (13) bone masses than do omnivores.

References

1. Food and Nutrition Board, National Research Council: *Recommended Dietary Allowances,* 10th ed. Washington, DC: National Academy Press, 1989.

2. Department of Health and Social Security: *Recommended Daily Amounts of Food Energy and Nutrients for Groups of People in the United Kingdom.* London: HMSO, 1979.

3. *Recommended Dietary Allowances for Japan.* Tokyo, Japan: Ministry of Health and Welfare, 1984.

4. Food and Nutrition Board, National Research Council: *Recommended Dietary Allowances,* 9th ed. Washington, DC: National Academy Press, 1980.

5. Zemel MB: Calcium utilization: Effect of varying level and source of dietary protein. *Am J Clin Nutr* 48: 880-883, 1988.

6. Kerstetter JE and Allen LH: Dietary protein increases urinary calcium. *J Nutr* 120: 134-136, 1990.

7. Linkswiler HM, Zemel MB, Hegsted M, Schuette S: Protein-induced hypercalciuria. *Fed Proc* 40: 2429-2433, 1981.

8. Roe LS, Thorogood M, Mann JI: Diet and plasma lipids in a group of vegetarians and omnivores. *Proc Nutr Soc* 49: 59A, 1990.

9. Kelsay JL: Update on fiber and mineral availability. In Vahouny GW and Kritchevsky D (eds): *Dietary Fiber.* New York: Plenum Publishing Corporation, 1986; 361-372.

10. Ellis FR et al: Incidence of osteoporosis in vegetarians and omnivores. *Am J Clin Nutr* 25: 555-558, 1972.

11. Hunt IF, Murphy NJ, Henderson C et al: Bone mineral content in postmenopausal women: comparison of omnivores and vegetarians. *Am J Clin Nutr* 50: 517-523, 1989.

12. Marsh AG, Sanchez TV, Chaffee FL et al: Bone mineral mass in adult lacto-ovo-vegetarian and omnivorous males. *Am J Clin Nutr 37: 453-456, 1983.*

13. Marsh AG, Sanchez TV, Mickelsen O et al: Cortical bone density of adult lacto-ovo-vegetarian and omnivorous women. *J Am Diet Assoc* 76: 148-151, 1980.

IRON

Summary: Dried beans and dark green vegetables are especially good sources of iron, better on a per calorie basis than meat. Iron absorption is increased markedly by eating foods containing vitamin C along with foods containing iron. Vegetarians do not have a higher incidence of iron deficiency than do meat eaters.

Iron is an essential nutrient because it is a central part of hemoglobin which carries oxygen in the blood. Iron deficiency anemia is a worldwide health problem which is especially common in young women and in children.

Iron is found in food in two forms, heme and non-heme iron. Heme iron, which makes up 40 percent of the iron in meat, poultry, and fish is well absorbed. Non-heme iron, 60 percent of the iron in animal tissue and all the iron in plants (fruits, vegetables, grains, nuts) is less well absorbed. Some might expect that since the vegan diet contains a form of iron which is not that well absorbed, vegans might be prone to developing iron deficiency anemia. However, recent surveys of vegans and vegetarians (1, 2, 3) have shown that iron deficiency anemia is no more common among vegetarians than among the general population.

The reason for the satisfactory iron status of many vegans may be that commonly eaten foods are high in iron, as Table 12 (page 164) shows. In fact, if the amount of iron in these foods is expressed as milligrams of iron per 100 calories, many foods eaten by vegans are superior to animal-derived foods. This concept is illustrated in Table 13 (page 166). For example, you would have to eat 340 calories of sirloin steak to get the same amount of iron as found in 100 calories of spinach.

Another reason for the satisfactory iron status of vegans is that vegan diets are high in vitamin C. Vitamin C acts to markedly increase absorption of non-heme iron. Adding a vitamin C source to a meal increases non-heme iron absorption up to six-fold which makes the absorption of non-heme iron as good or better than that of heme iron (4).

Fortunately, many vegetables, such as broccoli and bok choy, which are high in iron are also high in vitamin C so that the iron in these foods is very well absorbed. Commonly eaten combinations, such as beans and tomato sauce or stir-fried tofu and broccoli, also result in generous levels of iron absorption.

It is easy to obtain plenty of iron on a vegan diet. Table 14 (page 167) shows several menus which would meet the RDA (5) of 15 milligrams of iron per day for an adult woman. Men and post-menopausal women need about one-third less iron, 10 milligrams daily.

Some foods reduce iron absorption. Tea has tannin in it which binds iron in the intestines and decreases its absorption. Therefore, if you drink tea, drink it between meals. Herbal teas do not contain tannin and are an alternative to regular tea.

References

1. Anderson BM, Gibson RS, Sabry JH: The iron and zinc status of long-term vegetarian women. *Am J Clin Nutr* 34: 1042-1048, 1981.

2. Latta D and Liebman M: Iron and zinc status of vegetarian and non-vegetarian males. *Nutr Rep Int* 30: 141-149, 1984.

3. Helman AD and Darnton-Hill I: Vitamin and iron status in new vegetarians. *Am J Clin Nutr* 45: 785-789, 1987.

4. Hallberg L: Bioavailability of dietary iron in man. *Ann Rev Nutr* 1: 123-147, 1981.

5. Food and Nutrition Board, National Research Council: *Recommended Dietary Allowances*, 10th ed. Washington, DC: National Academy Press, 1989.

Table 12: Iron Content of Selected Vegan Foods

FOOD	AMOUNT	IRON (mg)
Tofu, firm	4 ounces	0.7-13.2
Soybeans, cooked	1 cup	8.8
Lentils, cooked	1 cup	6.6
Tofu, regular	4 ounces	0.7-6.6
Blackstrap molasses	2 TB	6.4
Quinoa, cooked	1 cup	5.3
Kidney beans, cooked	1 cup	5.2
Chickpeas, cooked	1 cup	4.7
Pinto beans, cooked	1 cup	4.5
Black-eyed peas, cooked	1 cup	4.3
Seitan	4 ounces	4.0
Swiss chard, cooked	1 cup	4.0
Tempeh	1 cup	3.8
Black beans, cooked	1 cup	3.6
Turnip greens, cooked	1 cup	3.2
Prune juice	8 ounces	3.0
Spinach, cooked	1 cup	2.9
Potato	1 medium	2.8
Beet greens, cooked	1 cup	2.7
Soy yogurt, plain	1 cup	2.7
Sesame seeds	2 TB	2.6
Tahini	2 TB	2.6
Peas, cooked	1 cup	2.5
Lima beans, cooked	1 cup	2.3
Sunflower seeds	1/4 cup	2.3
Figs, dried	5 medium	2.1
Cashews	1/4 cup	2.0
Apricots, dried	10 halves	2.0
Bulgur, cooked	1 cup	1.8
Bok choy, cooked	1 cup	1.8
Raisins	1/2 cup	1.6
Watermelon	1/8 medium	1.6

(Continued on next page.)

FOOD	AMOUNT	IRON (mg)
Soy milk, commercial, plain	8 ounces	1.5
Millet, cooked	1 cup	1.5
Tomato juice	8 ounces	1.4
Almonds	1/4 cup	1.3
Kale, cooked	1 cup	1.2
Brussels sprouts, cooked	1 cup	1.2
Broccoli, cooked	1 cup	1.1
Green beans, cooked	1 cup	1.1
Prunes	5 medium	1.0

Source: Composition of Foods, USDA Handbook 8.
Manufacturer's information.

The RDA for iron is 10 mg/day for adult men and for post-menopausal women and 15 mg/day for pre-menopausal women.

Table 13: Comparison of Iron Sources

Food	Iron (mg/100 calories)
Tofu, firm	7.1
Spinach, cooked	5.4
Collard greens, cooked	2.9
Lentils, cooked	2.9
Broccoli, cooked	2.2
Sirloin steak	1.6
Chickpeas, cooked	1.1
Figs, dried	0.9
Hamburger, cooked	0.8
Chicken, cooked	0.5
Pork Chop	0.4
Flounder, baked	0.3
Milk, skim	0.1

Note that the top iron sources are vegan.

Table 14: Sample Menus Providing More Than 15 milligrams of Iron

	Iron (mg)
Breakfast:	
1 svg Oatmeal Plus (p. 23)	3.8
Lunch:	
1 svg Tempeh/Rice Pocket Sandwich (p. 94)	4.7
10 Dried Apricots	2.0
Dinner:	
1 svg Black-Eyed Peas and Collards (p. 76)	2.1
1 svg Corn Bread (p. 21)	2.6
1 slice Watermelon	1.6
TOTAL	16.8

Breakfast:	
Cereal with 8 ounces of Soymilk	1.5
Lunch:	
Kidney Bean Chili (1 cup kidney beans)	5.2
1/4 cup Sunflower Seeds	2.3
Dinner:	
4 ounces Seitan stir-fried with	4.0
1 cup Bok Choy and sprinkled with	1.8
2 Tbsp Sesame Seeds	2.6
TOTAL	17.4

Additional foods should be added to these menus to provide adequate calories and to meet additional nutritional requirements.

ZINC

Summary: Zinc intakes of vegans are usually adequate since zinc is found in grains, legumes, and nuts.

Zinc is needed for growth, maturation, defense against infections, night vision, taste, and many other functions. The RDA for zinc is 15 milligrams per day for adult men and 12 milligrams per day for adult women (1). Intakes of zinc in the United States are generally between 10 and 15 milligrams daily (1, 2). One study examining Swedish vegans found similar levels of intake (3). Good sources of zinc include black-eyed peas, garbanzo beans, lentils, lima beans, green beans, oatmeal, brown rice, wheat germ, spinach, and nuts.

Phytate, a substance found in plant foods, has been shown to inhibit zinc absorption. However, phytate seems to have little influence on the amount of zinc which can be absorbed from American vegetarian diets unless the diet is very high in calcium (4). Vegan diets are seldom excessively high in calcium so it appears that phytate would only be a problem if high doses of calcium supplements were being used.

References

1. Food and Nutrition Board, National Research Council: *Recommended Dietary Allowances,* 10th ed. Washington, DC: National Academy Press, 1989.

2. Patterson KY, Holbrook JT, Bodner JE et al: Zinc, copper and manganese intake and balance for adults consuming self-selected diets. *Am J Clin Nutr* 40: 1397-1403, 1984.

3. Abdulla M, Andersson I, Asp N-G, et al: Nutrient intake and health status of vegans. Chemical analyses of diets using the duplicate portion sampling technique. *Am J Clin Nutr* 34: 2464-2477, 1981.

4. Ellis R, Kelsay JL, et al: Phytate:zinc and phytate x calcium:zinc millimolar ratios in self-selected diets of Americans, Asian Indians, and Nepalese. *J Am Diet Assoc* 87: 1043-1047, 1987.

VITAMIN D

Summary: Vitamin D is not found in the vegan diet but can be made by humans following exposure to sunlight. At least 10 to 15 minutes of summer sun on hands and face two or three times a week is recommended for adults so that vitamin D production can occur.

Vitamin D is essential for calcium absorption. Failure to obtain enough vitamin D is associated with bone disease in both adults and children. The vegan has no natural, reliable source of vitamin D in the diet. However, this should not be used to argue that we were meant to eat meat. Meat does not contain vitamin D either. In fact, the only naturally occurring sources of vitamin D are egg yolk and fatty fish. Vitamin D is added to cow's milk and butter in this country.

Vitamin D is unique among the vitamins because we can get it in other ways besides through diet. Vitamin D is first activated in the skin upon exposure to sunlight. It goes on to the liver and then to the kidney where it is converted into the form of vitamin D which regulates bone formation.

Adequate exposure to sunlight, 10 to 15 minutes of summer sun on hands and face two to three times a week, is recommended for adults to obtain adequate vitamin D (1). This recommendation is estimated from studies in infants. Those with darker skin and the elderly (2, 3) seem to require longer exposure to sunlight. Longer exposure is also needed in the winter. Sunscreens and air pollution also reduce the amount of vitamin D produced (4). Infants are also able to produce vitamin D after sunning (5). Throughout the year, infants should receive at least 2 hours a week of sunshine exposure to head and hands (1).

If you cannot routinely spend time outside and your diet has no vitamin D sources (eggs, cow's milk, fatty fish, butter), you may want to consider the use of a vitamin D supplement. The amount of vitamin D in the supplement should not be more than 5 micrograms (200 IU) for adults because high intakes of vitamin D can be toxic (6). Ergocalciferol, or vitamin D2, is a form of vitamin D which is not derived from animals.

References

1. Specker BL, Valanis B, Hertzberg V et al: Sunshine exposure and serum 25-hydroxyvitamin D concentrations in exclusively breast-fed infants. *J Pediatr* 107: 372-376, 1985.

2. Clemens TL, Henderson SL, Adams JS, Holick MF: Increased skin pigment reduces capacity of skin to synthesize vitamin D3. *Lancet* 1: 74-76, 1982.

3. Webb AR, Kline L, Holick MF: Influence of season and latitude on the cutaneous synthesis of vitamin D3: Exposure to winter sunlight in Boston and Edmonton will not promote vitamin D3 synthesis in human skin. *J Clin Endocrinol Metab* 67: 373-378, 1988.

4. Norman AW: Vitamin D. In Brown ML (ed): *Present Knowledge in Nutrition,* 6th ed. Washington, DC: International Life Sciences Institute, 1990; 108-116.

5. Specker BL and Tsang RC: Cyclical serum 25-hydroxyvitamin D concentrations paralleling sunshine exposure in exclusively breast-fed infants. *J Pediatr* 110: 744-747, 1987.

6. Food and Nutrition Board, National Research Council: *Recommended Dietary Allowances,* 10th ed. Washington, DC: National Academy Press, 1989.

RIBOFLAVIN AND VITAMIN B6

Summary: Adequate amounts of both riboflavin and vitamin B6 can be found in foods commonly eaten by vegans.

Riboflavin is a vitamin which has been mentioned as a potential problem for vegans. Superficially it would seem that vegan diets would be low in riboflavin since they do not contain what are considered major sources of riboflavin such as cow's milk, meat, and eggs. In reality, other good sources of riboflavin including wheat germ, soybeans, mushrooms, leafy green vegetables, avocados, nutritional yeast, and enriched breads and cereals are found in vegan diets. Thus, vegan diets can easily provide sufficient riboflavin.

Vitamin B6 has also been suggested to be problematic for vegans. At one point, pyridoxine glucoside, found in plant foods, was thought to reduce vitamin B6 availability (1). In other words, even though vegetables contained vitamin B6, they also appeared to contain pyridoxine glucoside which reduced the amount of vitamin B6 which could be absorbed. As is often the case, however, more complete study showed that pyridoxine glucoside did not impair vitamin B6 status in healthy humans (2). Good sources of vitamin B6 include brown rice, soybeans, oats, whole wheat bread, peanuts, and walnuts.

References

1. Reynolds RD: Bioavailability of vitamin B6 from plant foods. *Am J Clin Nutr* 48: 863-867, 1988.

2. Andon MB, Reynolds RD, Moser-Veillon PB, Howard MP: Dietary intake of total and glycosylated vitamin B6 and the vitamin B6 nutritional status of unsupplemented lactating women and their infants. *Am J Clin Nutr* 50: 1050-1058, 1989.

VITAMIN B12

Summary: The requirement for vitamin B12 is very low. Non-animal sources include Nutri-Grain cereal (1.4 ounces supplies the adult RDA) and Red Star T-6635+ nutritional yeast (1-2 teaspoons supplies the adult RDA). It is especially important for pregnant and lactating women, infants, and children to have reliable sources of vitamin B12 in their diets.

Vitamin B12 is needed for cell division and blood formation. Plant foods do not contain vitamin B12 except when they are contaminated by microorganisms. Thus, vegans need to look to other sources to get vitamin B12 in their diet. Although the minimum requirement for vitamin B12 is quite small, 1/1000 of a gram (1 microgram) a day for adults (1), a vitamin B12 deficiency is a very serious problem leading ultimately to irreversible nerve damage. Prudent vegans will include sources of vitamin B12 in their diets. However, vitamin B12 deficiency is actually quite rare even among long-term vegans.

Bacteria in the human intestinal tract do make vitamin B12. However, the majority of these bacteria are found in the large intestine. Vitamin B12 does not appear to be absorbed from the large intestine (2).

Normally, vitamin B12 is secreted into the small intestine along with bile and other secretions and is reabsorbed, but this does not add to the body's vitamin B12 stores. Since small amounts of vitamin B12 are not reabsorbed, it is possible that eventually vitamin B12 stores will be used up. However, we may be quite efficient at re-using vitamin B12 so that deficiency is rare.

Some bacteria in the small intestine apparently produce vitamin B12 (3) which can be absorbed (4). This is one possible explanation for why so few cases of vitamin B12 deficiency are reported. Perhaps our bacteria are making vitamin B12 for us.

At this time, research is continuing on vitamin B12 requirements. Some researchers have even hypothesized that vegans are more efficient than the general public in absorbing vitamin B12 (5). Certainly for other nutrients, such as iron, absorption is highest on low dietary intakes. However, these are only speculations. We need to look for reliable dietary sources for vitamin B12 until we can determine whether or not other sources can supply adequate vitamin B12.

Although some vegans may get vitamin B12 from inadequate hand washing, this is not a reliable vitamin B12 source. Vegans who previously ate animal-based foods may have vitamin B12 stores that will not be depleted for 20 to 30 years (2) or more. However, long-term vegans, infants, children, and pregnant and lactating women (due to increased needs) should be especially careful to get enough vitamin B12.

Few reliable vegan food sources for vitamin B12 are known. Tempeh, miso, and seaweed often are labeled as having large amounts of vitamin B12. However, these products are not reliable sources of the vitamin because the amount of vitamin B12 present depends on the type of processing the food undergoes (2, 6). Also, Victor Herbert, a leading authority on vitamin B12 states that the amount on the label cannot be trusted because the current method for measuring vitamin B12 in foods measures both active and inactive forms of vitamin B12. The inactive form (also called analogues) actually interferes with normal vitamin B12 absorption and metabolism (2, 7). These foods may contain more inactive than active vitamin B12.

At least one brand of nutritional yeast, Red Star T-6635+, has been tested and shown to contain active vitamin B12. This brand of yeast is a reliable source of vitamin B12. Nutritional yeast, Saccharomyces cerevisiae, is a food yeast, grown on a molasses solution, which comes as yellow flakes or powder. It has a cheesy taste. Nutritional yeast is different from brewer's yeast or torula yeast. It can often be used by those sensitive to other yeasts.

The RDA (which includes a safety factor) for adults for vitamin B12 is 2 micrograms daily (1). Two micrograms of vitamin B12 are provided by 1 teaspoon of Red Star T-6635+ yeast powder or 1-1/2 teaspoons of mini-flake yeast or 2 rounded teaspoons of large-flake yeast. Of course, since vitamin B12 is stored, you could use larger amounts of nutritional yeast less often. A number of the recipes in this book contain nutritional yeast.

Another alternative source of vitamin B12 is fortified cereal. Nutri-Grain cereal does contain vitamin B12 at this time and 1.4 ounces of Nutri-Grain, or a little less than 1 cup, will provide 2 micrograms of vitamin B12. We recommend checking the label of your favorite cereal since manufacturers have been known to stop including vitamin B12. New labeling laws do not require labels to include the actual amount of vitamin B12 in a food. However, added vitamin B12 will be listed under ingredients and you can write to the company inquiring about the amount of vitamin B12 in a serving.

Other sources of vitamin B12 are fortified soy milk (check the label as this is rarely available in the US), vitamin B12 fortified meat analogues (food made from wheat gluten or soybeans to resemble meat, poultry or fish), and vitamin B12 supplements. There are vitamin supplements which do not contain animal products.

References

1. Food and Nutrition Board, National Research Council: *Recommended Dietary Allowances,* 10th ed. Washington, DC: National Academy Press, 1989.

2. Herbert V: Vitamin B12: Plant sources, requirements, and assay. *Am J Clin Nutr* 48: 852-858, 1988.

3. Albert MJ, Mathan VI, Baker SJ: Vitamin B12 synthesis by human small intestinal bacteria. *Nature* 283: 781-782, 1980.

4. Herbert VD and Colman N: Folic acid and vitamin B12. In Shils ME and Young VR (eds): *Modern Nutrition in Health and Disease,* 7th ed. Philadelphia: Lea and Febiger, 1988; 388-416.

5. Immerman AM: Vitamin B12 status on a vegetarian diet. A critical review. *Wld Rev Nutr Diet* 37: 38-54, 1981.

6. Specker BL, Miller D, Norman EJ et al: Increased urinary methylmalonic acid excretion in breast-fed infants of vegetarian mothers and identification of an acceptable dietary source of vitamin B12. *Am J Clin Nutr* 47: 89-92, 1987.

7. Kondo H, Binder MJ, Kohhouse JF et al: Presence and formation of cobalamin analogues in multivitamin-mineral pills. *J Clin Invest* 70: 889-898, 1982.

SOURCES OF VITAMINS AND MINERALS

Other vitamins and minerals are generally easy to obtain from a varied diet. Good sources for essential vitamins and minerals are listed below.

Vitamin A - carrots, winter squash, sweet potatoes, apricots, peaches, spinach, kale, greens, broccoli

Vitamin D - exposure to sunlight

Vitamin E - vegetable oils, margarine, wheat germ, nuts

Vitamin K - green leafy vegetables, cauliflower

Thiamin - grains, cereals, brewer's yeast, nutritional yeast, legumes, seeds, nuts

Riboflavin - enriched breads and cereals, nutritional yeast, wheat germ, soybeans, mushrooms, broccoli, turnip greens, asparagus, spinach, avocados

Niacin - breads, cereals, legumes, green vegetables

Vitamin B6 - brown rice, soybeans, oats, whole wheat products, peanuts, walnuts, bananas

Folacin - green leafy vegetables, legumes, nuts, oranges

Vitamin B12 - nutritional yeast, vitamin B12 fortified cereals, vitamin B12 fortified soy milk

Biotin - soy flour, cereals, yeast

Pantothenic Acid - whole grain cereals, legumes

(Continued on next page.)

Vitamin C - green and red peppers, collard greens, broccoli, spinach, brussels sprouts, tomatoes, potatoes, strawberries, oranges, grapefruit, orange juice, melon

Calcium - broccoli, kale, collard greens, calcium-precipitated tofu, blackstrap molasses, bok choy

Phosphorus - cereal grains, nuts, dried beans, peas, lentils

Iron - green leafy vegetables, dried beans and legumes, blackstrap molasses, dried fruits, watermelon

Magnesium - nuts, legumes, unmilled grains, green vegetables, bananas

Zinc - black-eyed peas, garbanzo beans, lentils, lima beans, green peas, oatmeal, brown rice, spinach, nuts, wheat germ

Iodine - iodized salt, commercial bread, sea vegetables, plants depending on soil iodine content

Selenium - grains and legumes depending on soil selenium content

Manganese - whole grains and cereals, tea, nuts, legumes

Fluoride - fluoridated water, tea

Chromium - brewer's yeast, whole grains

Molybdenum - beans, breads, cereals

PREGNANCY AND THE VEGAN DIET

Pregnancy is a time of increased nutritional needs, both to support the rapidly growing fetus and to allow for the changes occurring in the pregnant woman's body. Throughout pregnancy, recommended intakes of many vitamins and minerals are higher than those recommended prior to pregnancy. For example, the recommendation for folic acid is more than doubled and the recommendation for calcium is 50% higher during pregnancy (1).

How can you meet these increased needs by following a vegan diet? A series of studies (2, 3) at The Farm, a community where vegan diets are a part of a socially responsible life-style, have shown that vegans can have healthy pregnancies and that infants and children can safely follow a vegan diet.

Although recommendations for many vitamins and minerals are higher in pregnancy, the increase in energy (calorie) requirements is relatively small. For this reason, some care and thought are needed by all pregnant women to insure that nutritional needs are met.

If you are newly pregnant or are considering becoming pregnant, take a minute and ask yourself some questions. Your answers to these questions will affect some of the choices that you make with regard to diet and life-style in pregnancy.

1. What is your pre–pregnant weight? How tall are you?

Your answer to these questions can be used to decide if you are underweight or overweight. To determine this, use Table 15 (page 178) to calculate your body mass index (BMI) and your weight-for-height status. If you have a moderate BMI, a weight gain of 25-35 pounds during pregnancy is recommended (4). If your BMI is low or very low, you should gain more weight, 28-40 pounds. If your BMI is high or very high, you still should gain at least 15 pounds.

Table 15. Body Mass Index

Step 1. Take your prepregnant weight (in pounds) and divide it by your height (in inches) squared; then multiply by 700. BMI = lb/in² x 700. For example, if I weigh 110 pounds and am 60 inches tall, my BMI is 110/3600 x 700 = 21.4.

Step 2. Use your BMI to find your pre-pregnancy weight-for-height status and the amount of weight you should try to gain in pregnancy.

BMI	Weight-for-height status	Recommended weight gain
<19.8	Low	28-40 pounds
19.8 to 26	Average	25-35 pounds
26 to 29	High	15-25 pounds
>29	Very high	no less than 15 pounds

Adapted from reference 4.

Young adolescents and black women should attempt to gain at the upper end of the given ranges since these groups tend to have higher rates of low birth weight infants. Higher weight gains seem to reduce the risk of having an infant whose weight at birth is very low and who is at risk for complications. Short women (under 62 inches) should attempt to gain at the lower end of the given ranges.

The pattern of weight gain is different for each woman. However, a general trend is to have little weight gain for the first 12 weeks. Then, in the second and third trimesters, a weight gain of a pound a week is common. Figure 1 (page 180) shows recommended patterns of weight gain based on your pre-pregnancy body mass index. Select the graph corresponding to your pre-pregnant BMI. Your weight gain will not necessarily fall on the dashed line but should be approximately parallel to the line (4).

If you are gaining weight very slowly or not gaining weight at all, you will need to eat more food. Perhaps eating more often or eating food somewhat higher in fat and lower in bulk will help. If your weight gain seems high, consider the types of foods you are eating. If you are eating a lot of sweet or fatty foods, replace them with fruits, vegetables, grains, and legumes. If your diet already seems healthy, try to get more exercise -- walk or swim daily, for example. Of course, you should discuss your exercise regimen with your health care provider. Remember, each woman, and more precisely, each pregnancy, is different in terms of weight gain.

In order to support the recommended weight gain, you will need about 300 calories more than usual in the second and third trimesters (1). There is little, if any, increase in calorie needs in the first three months of pregnancy. Three hundred calories is a fairly small increase compared to the increases seen for other nutrients, so it is important to use those calories wisely. In other words, instead of drinking two cans of soda (300 calories, but not good nutritionally) you could eat 300 calories worth of fruits and vegetables and meet your needs for many vitamins and minerals. Table 16 (page 183) shows some ways of getting an extra 300 calories.

Your best guide for how much you should be eating is your own body. If you select healthy foods, exercise moderately, and eat regularly, your feelings of hunger should let you know when and how much to eat.

2. What is your usual pattern of eating? For example, do you skip breakfast and lunch and eat a big dinner or do you nibble all day?

The answer to question 2 can give you some ideas for adapting your usual eating patterns to insure that you are getting enough food. If you usually skip breakfast and/or lunch, it will be difficult or impossible to eat enough food at one or two meals to meet your needs. Also, babies do not do well with fasting for any length of time. Many women find that it works best to eat small

Figure 1: Weight Gain in Pregnancy

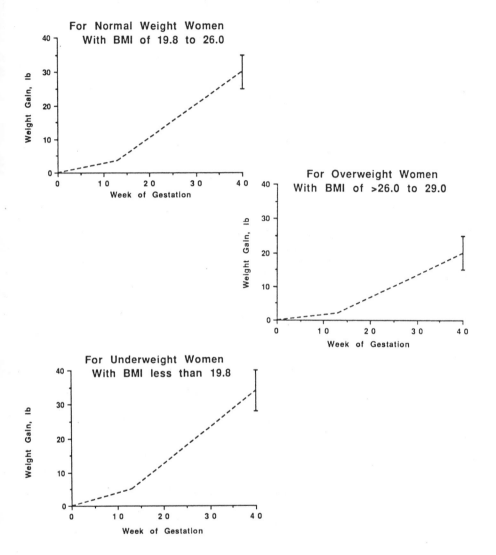

Source: Adapted from Reference 4.

Select the graph corresponding to pre-pregnancy BMI. Weight gain will not necessarily fall on the dashed line but should approximately parallel the line. The vertical line at the right of each graph shows the range of recommended weight gain.

meals frequently, especially during the last few months of pregnancy, when there just doesn't seem to be enough room for food. This is especially true for vegans, whose diets are higher in fiber and bulk, making it harder for them to eat a lot at one time. Small, frequent meals can also help with low weight gain. Don't feel like you have to actually prepare a meal six times a day. A meal can be as simple as a bowl of cereal, soy yogurt and fruit, peanut butter and crackers, or almonds and raisins.

3. How "good" is your diet? Do you eat grains, legumes, fruits, and vegetables every day?

Your answer to question 3 can help you to decide whether your current diet meets the nutritional recommendations for pregnancy.

The newest recommendations for protein needs in pregnancy are lower than previous recommendations. The current RDA for protein in pregnancy is 60 grams per day (1). This is 10 grams above the recommendation for non-pregnant women age 25-50 and 14 grams above the recommendation for non-pregnant women age 19-24 years. If your diet is varied and contains good protein sources such as soy products, beans, and grains, you can relax and not worry about getting enough protein in pregnancy. Some ways that you can get another 10-15 grams of protein within the extra 300 calories are: 2 cups of plain soy milk, 9 ounces of tofu, 3 ounces of tempeh, 1 cup of cooked beans, 1-1/2 bagels. This is in addition to the protein which normally occurs in your diet. Making sure you have enough calories insures that the protein you eat is used for tissue synthesis rather than meeting energy needs.

Other important nutrients in pregnancy include calcium, vitamin D, iron, vitamin B12, zinc, and folic acid.

Calcium and vitamin D both are needed for bone and tooth development. Calcium absorption is high in pregnancy (5), so if your diet is slightly low in calcium, your body may automatically compensate for it. There is little evidence of calcium loss from the mother's bones during pregnancy and no adverse effects of diets low in calcium during pregnancy have been reported (4). However, since low calcium intakes are not recommended during the years when women are accumulating bone mass, an intake of 1200 milligrams per day is recommended for women under age 25 (1, 4). Intakes of between 600 and 1200 milligrams per day of calcium have been recommended for pregnant women age 25 and older (1, 4). Vegans may need less calcium than omnivores because the vegan diet may result in lower losses of calcium due to the lower protein nature of the diet.

During pregnancy, eating four or more servings of calcium-rich foods daily is recommended. Ideas for these foods include greens, tofu processed with calcium sulfate, and blackstrap molasses. Try snacking on tahini spread on toast or eat some figs. Take a box of frozen greens (spinach, collards, kale, etc.) to work and heat it in the microwave for a calcium-rich afternoon snack. Calcium supplements represent another option for those days when your appetite is poor or you don't have time to prepare foods. You should be aware, however, that calcium supplements can cause constipation.

Vitamin D, which is produced following exposure of skin to sunlight, is not normally found in foods eaten by vegans. Pregnant vegans should be sure to get at least 20 to 30 minutes of summer sun on their hands and face two to three times a week (6). Vitamin D supplementation should be undertaken only with the approval of your physician, since excess vitamin D is toxic and can produce fetal deformities. A vitamin D supplement of 10 micrograms (400 IU) daily should be taken by pregnant vegans who live at northern latitudes in the winter (due to reduced intensity of sunlight) and by those with minimal exposure to sunlight (for example, those who work indoors during daylight hours) (4).

Extra iron is needed in pregnancy to provide for increased maternal blood volume and for the formation of the baby's blood. If the mother does not have enough iron in her diet, she will draw on her iron stores and can become anemic. The RDA for iron in pregnancy is 30 milligrams per day (1) which is difficult (although not impossible) to get on any diet. See the iron section (pages 162-167) for a list of foods especially high in iron.

Recent recommendations (4) support the routine use of a supplement of 30 milligrams of ferrous iron daily during the second and third trimester in addition to dietary iron. You should discuss iron supplementation with your health care provider. If there is evidence that you are anemic, supplementation with 60 to 120 milligrams per day of ferrous iron is recommended (4). The iron supplement that you take should be taken only in combination with a good diet. Doses of iron above these recommendations can interfere with zinc and copper absorption (7-9) and so should be avoided, if possible.

Table 16: 300 Calorie Snacks

1 serving Fruit Whiz (p. 17)
1 serving Pita Chips (p. 36)

2 Apple Raisin Spice Muffins (p. 20)
1/2 cup Soy Milk

1 serving Hummus Spread (p. 27) on
1 slice Whole Wheat Bread

1 serving Cheesy Pita Toast (p. 37)
1 cup Apple Juice

1 serving Tofu Dip (p. 99) with
Fresh Vegetables

3 Ginger Cookies (p. 109)
1 cup Soy Milk

1 serving Karen's Creamy Rice Pudding (p. 115)
1 large Apple

1 cup Soy Yogurt with
2 Tbsp Nuts and Dried Fruit

1 Bagel with
1 Tbsp Almond Butter

1 serving Thick Shake (p. 18)

Vitamin B12 needs are higher in pregnancy due to vitamin B12's role in tissue synthesis. If you are planning to breast feed, you will also need to make sure that you have enough vitamin B12 stored so that your milk vitamin B12 will be high enough to meet the infant's needs. At least one brand of nutritional yeast, Red Star T-6635+, has been tested and shown to contain active vitamin B12. This brand of yeast is a reliable source of vitamin B12. The RDA for pregnancy for vitamin B12 is 2.2 micrograms daily. A rounded teaspoon of Red Star T-6635+ yeast powder or 2 teaspoons of mini-flake yeast or 2-1/2 teaspoons of large-flake yeast provides 2.2 micrograms of vitamin B12. Of course, since vitamin B12 is stored, you could consume larger amounts of nutritional yeast less often. Another alternative source of vitamin B12 is fortified cereal. Nutri-Grain cereal contains vitamin B12 at this time. 2.2 micrograms of vitamin B12 are provided by 1.5 ounces (about 1 cup) of wheat Nutri-Grain. Check the label of your favorite cereal because manufacturers have been known to stop including vitamin B12. Other sources of vitamin B12 are fortified soy milk (check the label as this is rarely available in the US), vitamin B12 fortified meat analogues (food made from wheat gluten or soybeans to resemble meat, poultry or fish), and vitamin B12 supplements. There are vitamin supplements that do not contain animal products.

Zinc is a mineral which is necessary for growth and development. In fact, the recommendation for zinc during pregnancy is twice as high as for non-pregnant women. Good sources of zinc include legumes, grains, and nuts. Folic acid is another nutrient whose requirement appears to be substantially increased in pregnancy. Dark leafy greens are the richest source of folic acid for vegans. Other good sources include whole grains, nuts, legumes, and oranges.

4. Do you drink alcohol regularly? Do you smoke? What about caf-feine?

Moderate to large amounts of alcohol during pregnancy can cause fetal alcohol syndrome, which impairs mental and physical development. Even one or two drinks of alcohol are associated with greater risk of spontaneous abortion and low birth weight (10). Based on what we know, the current recommendation is that women should avoid alcohol during pregnancy (10). Cigarette smoking has been clearly linked to low birth weight, which increases the infant's chance of having a variety of health problems. Smoking should also be avoided during pregnancy.

Caffeine is more controversial. Large amounts have, in some cases, been associated with various problems in pregnancy (10). Caffeine does appear in the fetus's blood in the same concentration as in the mother's blood. It is probably wisest to limit or avoid caffeine-containing beverages such as coffee, tea, and cola.

5. How old are you?

If you are a teenager, you will need extra food so that your growth can continue even while you are pregnant. You should be especially careful to get plenty of good quality food, have an adequate (more than 25 pound) weight gain, and get early prenatal care.

Morning Sickness

Morning sickness is a common complaint, especially early in pregnancy. Each woman has a variety of ideas for controlling nausea. Try these suggestions and see what works for you:

● Eat 5 or 6 small meals a day. Try to eat something every few hours because you may feel sick when you are really hungry.

● Avoid greasy or fried foods, as these take longer to digest.

● If the smell of cooking makes you queasy, ask someone else to cook while you are out of the house or try eating cold foods like sandwiches, cereal, soy yogurt, nut or seed butter and crackers, or fruit.

● Don't lie down right after you eat.

● Keep a snack like crackers or dry cereal by your bed and eat a little if you wake up in the night or before you get up in the morning.

● Try making mixtures like mashed potatoes and chopped vegetables or vegetables and rice, because starchy foods are often more appealing than vegetables.

● Be sure to drink juice, water, fruit smoothies, soy milk, or miso broth if you can't eat solid food. Keep trying to eat whatever you can.

Constipation

Constipation is also a common complaint. It occurs because of hormonal changes associated with pregnancy and is often worsened by calcium or iron supplements. Vegans may not have as much of a problem with this because of the high fiber nature of their diet. If it is a problem for you, be sure to drink plenty of liquid, walk every day, eat dried fruits like raisins and prunes (also a good iron source), and eat fruits, vegetables, and whole grains.

Several diet guides have been produced for pregnant vegans. While our recommendation is generally to eat a varied diet containing foods high in the nutrients needed during pregnancy, some people feel more comfortable with a more structured guide for daily eating.

Here are two different meal plans for pregnant vegans (11):

PLAN I	QUANTITY
NUTS, SEEDS, OR LEGUMES	● 2 servings (a serving is 2 TB nuts or seeds or 1/2 cup cooked legumes)
MILK OR MEAT ANALOGS	● 3 servings (1 cup soymilk is a serving)
VEGETABLES	● 4 servings (a serving is 1 cup raw or 1/2 cup cooked). We suggest emphasizing high calcium vegetables such as greens and broccoli.
FRUITS	● 5 servings (a serving is 1 fruit or 1/2 cup canned fruit or juice).
GRAINS, CEREALS, OR BREADS	● 6 servings (a serving is 1 slice of bread or 1/2 cup cereal or grain)

PLAN II	QUANTITY
LEGUMES	● 4 servings
MILK OR MEAT ANALOGUES	● 4 servings
VEGETABLES AND FRUITS	● 8 servings. We suggest emphasizing high calcium vegetables such as greens and broccoli.
GRAINS, CEREALS, OR BREADS	● 6 servings

References

1. Food and Nutrition Board, National Research Council: *Recommended Dietary Allowances,* 10th ed. Washington, DC: National Academy Press, 1989.

2. O'Connell JM, Dibley MJ, Sierra J, et al: Growth of vegetarian children: The Farm study. *Pediatrics* 84: 475-481, 1989.

3. Carter JP, Furman T, Hutcheson HR: Preeclampsia and reproductive performance in a community of vegans. *Southern Med J* 80: 692-697, 1987.

4. Institute of Medicine Subcommittee on Nutritional Status and Weight Gain During Pregnancy: *Nutrition During Pregnancy.* Washington, DC: National Academy Press, 1990.

5. Heaney RP and Skillman TG: Calcium metabolism in human pregnancy. *J Clin Endocrinol Metab* 33: 661-670, 1971.

6. Specker BL, Valanis B, Hertzberg V et al: Sunshine exposure and serum 25-hydroxyvitamin D concentrations in exclusively breast-fed infants. *J Pediatr* 107: 372-376, 1985.

7. Solomons NW: Competitive interaction of iron and zinc in the diet: Consequences for human nutrition. *J Nutr* 116: 927-935, 1986.

8. Hambidge KM, Krebs NF, Sibley L et al: Acute effects of iron therapy on zinc status during pregnancy. *Obstet Gynecol* 4: 593-596, 1987.

9. Dawson EB, Albers J, McGanity WJ: Serum zinc changes due to iron supplementation in teenage pregnancy. *Am J Clin Nutr* 50: 848-852, 1989.

10. US Department of Health and Human Services: *The Surgeon General's Report on Nutrition and Health.* Washington, DC: US Government Printing Office, 1988.

11. Johnston PK: Counseling the pregnant vegetarian. *Am J Clin Nutr* 48: 901-905, 1988.

LACTATION AND THE VEGAN DIET

The best diet for breast feeding is very similar to the diet recommended for pregnancy. Calories, protein, and vitamin B12 recommendations are higher while the recommendation for iron is lower than during pregnancy.

If you eat too little while breast feeding, you may not produce as much milk. Although the recommended calorie intake is 500 calories above your usual intake (1), you still may lose weight because of a loss of calories in breast milk. It is safe to lose about 1/2 to 1 pound a week while breast feeding but more rigorous dieting is not recommended. As in pregnancy, small frequent meals are the best way to be sure that you are getting enough calories. Since you do need extra fluid while breast feeding, use nutritious beverages like juices, soy milk, soups, and smoothies to provide calories.

The recommendation for protein is only 5 grams higher than it is in pregnancy (1) and can be obtained easily from the extra food you are eating. You should still eat good quality food because you are providing all nutrients to your infant. You will need to be careful to get enough vitamin B12 and vitamin D in order to be sure that these nutrients are present in your milk in adequate amounts. See the Pregnancy section (pages 177-187) for more information on sources of vitamin B12 and vitamin D. Requirements for most other nutrients are similar to those in pregnancy and should be obtained from a varied, healthy vegan diet.

Reference

1. Food and Nutrition Board, National Research Council: *Recommended Dietary Allowances,* 10th ed. Washington, DC: National Academy Press, 1989.

FEEDING VEGAN KIDS

Many members of The Vegetarian Resource Group are glowing testimony to the fact that vegan children can be healthy, grow normally, be extremely active and (we think) smarter than average. Of course it takes time and thought to feed vegan children. Shouldn't feeding of any child require time and thought? After all, the years from birth to adolescence are the years when eating habits are set, when growth rate is high, and to a large extent, when the size of stores of essential nutrients such as calcium and iron are determined.

The earliest food for a vegan baby should be either breast milk or soy formula. A wonderful trend in this country is that breast feeding is on the rise. Many benefits to the infant are conveyed by breast feeding including some enhancement of the immune system, protection against infection, and reduced risk of allergies. In addition, breast milk was designed for baby humans and quite probably contains substances needed by growing infants which are not even known to be essential and are not included in infant formulas. If you choose to breast feed, be sure to see the preceding section on lactation to make sure that your milk is adequate for your child. Be especially careful that you are getting enough vitamin B12 and that your infant receives at least 2 hours a week of sunshine exposure to head and hands (1). Vitamin D supplements of 400 IU per day are recommended for breast fed infants age three months and older receiving limited sunshine exposure (2). Because vitamin D deficiency leads to rickets (soft, improperly mineralized bones) and because vitamin D is found only in very low amounts in human milk, if there is any question about whether or not your infant gets enough sun (cloudy climate, winter, dark-skinned infant), vitamin D supplements are a wise idea. No other supplements are usually needed for the first 6 months. Iron supplementation is often started for breast fed infants at 6 months.

Many books on infant care (see Recommended Reading list page 204) have sections on techniques and timing of breast feeding, and we suggest that you refer to one of these for more information. Be forewarned that they may discourage vegetarianism. They are wrong. With a little attention to detail, vegetarianism and breast feeding are a good combination. In fact, at least one report shows that milk of vegetarian women is lower in pesticides than the milk of women eating typical American diets (3).

If for any reason you choose not to breast feed or if you are using formula to supplement breast feeding, there are several soy-based formulas available. Brand names include Isomil[R], Prosobee[R], Nursoy[R], and Soyalac[R]. These formulas can be used exclusively for the first 6 months. Iron supplements may be indicated at 4 months if the formula is not supplemented with iron.

Soy milk should not be substituted for soy formula in infants. Soy milk does not contain the proper ratio of protein, fat, and carbohydrate nor does it have enough of many vitamins and minerals to be used as the only food or almost only food an infant receives.

Supplemental food (food besides breast milk and formula) can be started at different times in different children depending on the child's rate of growth and stage of development. Some signs of the time to start introducing solid foods are: when the baby has doubled in weight since birth or weighs about 13 pounds AND when a breast fed baby demands to be fed more than 8-10 times in 24 hours or the formula fed baby consistently drinks more than a quart of formula per day AND when the baby often seems hungry (4). Usually these signs occur when the child is developmentally ready to begin solid foods.

Introduce one new food at a time to reduce the risk of allergy. Many people use iron-fortified infant rice cereal as the first food. This is a good choice as it is a good source of iron and rice cereal is least likely to cause an allergic response. Cereal can be mixed with expressed breast milk or soy formula so the consistency is fairly thin. Formula or breast milk feedings should continue as usual. Start with one cereal feeding daily and work up to 2 meals daily or 1/3 to 1/2 cup. Oats, barley, corn, and other grains can be ground in a blender and then cooked until very soft and smooth. These cereals can be introduced one at a time. However, they do not contain much iron, so iron supplements should be continued.

Once the baby is familiar with cereals (6-8 months), fruit, fruit juice, and vegetables can be introduced. Mashed banana is one food that many infants especially enjoy. Other fruits include mashed avocado, applesauce, and pureed canned peaches or pears. Citrus fruits and juices should be introduced after the fifth month. Mild vegetables (such as potatoes, carrots, peas, sweet potatoes, and green beans) should be cooked well and mashed. There is no need to add spices, sugar, or salt to cereals, fruits, and vegetables. Crackers, pieces of bread, and dry cereal can be introduced between 6 and 8 months.

By 7-10 months table foods can be introduced. Tofu is a good choice to provide protein, iron, and calcium (choose tofu processed with calcium sulfate). By this time your child can progress from mashed or pureed food to pieces of soft food. Continued use of iron-fortified infant cereals is recommended until at least 18 months.

By 10-12 months, your child should be eating at least the amounts of foods shown in Table 17 (page 192).

Certainly it makes sense for vegans to continue breast feeding for a year or longer, if possible, because breast milk is a rich source of nutrients. However, many infants are not that interested in breast feeding after 10-12 months and will begin drinking from a cup. What should go into that cup? Ideally a fortified soy formula should be used until around age 6. *Laurel's Kitchen* (5) gives a recipe for fortified soy milk that can be prepared at home. Commercial soy milks are another option. However, in this country, they are seldom fortified with vitamins and minerals so if soy milk is used, more care must be taken to insure that the child's diet is adequate.

Several studies have been reported showing that the growth of vegan children is slower than that of non-vegans (see 6-8). Studies such as these are often cited as evidence that vegan diets are inherently unhealthy. However, when the studies are examined more closely, we find that they are often based on vegans who have very low calorie or very limited diets (only fruit and nuts for example).

An additional question that must be asked is, "What is a normal growth rate?" Growth rate is assessed by comparing changes in a child's height, weight, and head circumference to rates of growth that have been established by measuring large numbers of apparently healthy US children. There is no one ideal rate of growth. Instead, height, weight, and head circumference are reported in percentiles. If your child's height is at the 50th percentile, this means that 50% of children of that age are taller and 50% are shorter. Similarly, a weight at the 25th percentile means 25% of children weigh less and 75% weigh more.

Table 17: Feeding Schedule For Vegan Babies Ages 6–12 Months

	4-7 mos [*]	6-8 mos	7-10 mos	10-12 mos
MILK	Breast milk or soy formula.	Breast milk or soy formula.	Breast milk or soy formula.	Breast milk or soy formula (16–24 ounces).
CEREAL & BREAD	Begin iron-fortified baby cereal mixed with milk.	Continue baby cereal. Begin other breads and cereals.	Baby cereal. Other breads and cereals.	Baby cereal until 18 mos. Total of 4 svgs (1 svg=1/4 slice bread or 2-4 TB cereal).
FRUITS & VEGETABLES	None	Begin juice from cup: 3 oz vit C source. Begin mashed vegetables & fruits.	3 oz juice. Pieces of soft/cooked fruits & vegetables.	Table-food diet. Allow 4 svgs per day (1 svg=1-6 TB fruit & vegetable, 3 oz juice).
LEGUMES & NUTS	None	None	Gradually introduce tofu. Begin casseroles, peanut butter, other nut butters, legumes, soy cheese, & soy yogurt.	2 svgs daily each about 1/2 oz.

Adapted from (10) and (13).

*Overlap of ages occurs because of varying rate of development.

While some studies show that vegan children are at a lower percentile of weight and height than are other children of a similar age, a recent study shows that vegan children can have growth rates which do not differ from those of omnivorous children of the same age (9). At this time we cannot say that a child growing at the 25th percentile is any more or less healthy than a child growing at the 75th percentile. What seems to be more important is that the child stays at about the same percentile. For example, a child who is at the 50th percentile for height at age 2 and only at the 25th percentile at age 3 has had a faltering in growth rate. The cause of this faltering should be determined.

The best way to assure that your children achieve their ideal rate of growth is to make sure that they have adequate calories. Some vegan children have difficulty getting enough calories because of the sheer bulk of their diets. Children have small stomachs and can become full before they have eaten enough food to sustain growth. The judicious use of fats in forms like avocados, nuts, nut butters, seeds, and seed butters will provide a concentrated source of calories needed by many vegan children. Dried fruits are also a concentrated calorie source and are an attractive food for many children. Teeth should be brushed after eating dried fruits to prevent tooth decay.

Diets of young children should not be overly high in fiber since this may limit the amount of food they can eat. The fiber content of a vegan child's diet can be reduced by giving the child some refined grain products, fruit juices, and peeled vegetables.

Sources of protein for vegan children include legumes, grains, tofu, tempeh, soymilk, nuts, peanut butter, tahini, soy hot dogs, soy yogurt, and soy cheese. Some of these foods should be used daily. Children should get enough calories so that protein can be used for growth in addition to meeting energy needs.

Table 18 (page 194) shows one diet plan that has been used successfully by vegan children (adapted from 10, 11).

Table 18: Diet Plan For Vegan Children

FOOD	1-4 yrs	4-6 yrs	7-12 yrs
BREAD	3 slices	4 slices	4-5 slices
CEREALS & GRAINS	1/2 cup	1 cup	1 cup
NUTS, NUT BUTTER, LEGUMES, TOFU	3 TB-1 cup	3 TB-1 cup	3 TB-1-1/2 cups
FATS	3 tsp	4 tsp	5 tsp
FRUITS			
CITRUS	1/2-1 cup juice or chopped	1/2-1 cup	1/2-1 cup
OTHER	1/4-3/4 cup chopped	1/2-1 cup	1-1-1/2 cups
VEGETABLES			
LEAFY GREEN OR YELLOW	2-3 TB chopped	1/4-1/3 cup	1/2-1 cup
OTHER	1/4-1/3 cup chopped	1/4-1/3 cup	1-1-1/2 cups
SOYMILK	3 cups	3 cups	3-4 cups
NUTRITIONAL YEAST	1 TB	1 TB	1 TB
BLACKSTRAP MOLASSES	1 TB	1 TB	1 TB

Adapted from (10) and (11).

The calorie content of the diet can be increased by greater amounts of nut butters, dried fruits, and cereals.

The nutritional yeast should be fortified with vitamin B12 (check the label) and a vitamin B12-fortified cereal should be used often or vitamin B12 supplements are recommended.

If the soy milk is not fortified with calcium, other sources of calcium such as leafy green vegetables and tofu processed with calcium sulfate should be used.

This plan may be low in zinc unless wheat germ or fortified cereals are used.

Adequate exposure to sunlight, 20 to 30 minutes of summer sun on hands and face two to three times a week, is recommended to promote vitamin D synthesis (1).

Although today more and more children are vegan from birth, many older children also become vegan. There are many ways to make a transition from a non-vegan to a vegan diet. Some families gradually eliminate dairy products and eggs, while others make a more abrupt transition. Regardless of which approach you choose, be sure to explain to your child what is going on and why, at your child's level. Offer foods that look familiar, at first. Peanut butter sandwiches seem to be universally popular and many children like pasta or tacos. Gradually introduce new foods. Watch your child's weight closely. If weight loss occurs or the child doesn't seem to be growing as rapidly, add more concentrated calories and reduce the fiber in your child's diet.

Teenage vegans have nutritional needs that are the same as any other teenager. The years between 13 and 19 are times of especially rapid growth and change. Nutritional needs are high during these years. The teenage vegan should follow the same recommendations that are made for all vegans, namely to eat a wide variety of foods, including fruits, vegetables, plenty of leafy greens, whole grain products, nuts, seeds, and legumes. Protein, calcium, iron, and vitamin B12 are nutrients teenage vegans should be aware of.

The recommendation for protein is 0.5 grams per pound for 11-14 year olds and 0.4 grams per pound for 15-18 year olds (12). Those exercising strenuously (marathon runners, for example) may need _slightly_ more protein. A 16 year old who weighs 120 pounds, needs about 44 grams of protein daily. In terms of food, 1 cup of cooked dried beans has 14 grams of protein, a cup of soy milk or soy yogurt has 8-10 grams, 4 ounces of tofu has 9 grams, a tablespoon of peanut butter or peanuts has 4 grams, and 1 slice of bread or 1 cup of grain has about 3 grams.

Fruits, fats, and alcohol do not provide much protein, and so a diet based only on these foods would have a good chance of being too low in protein. Vegans eating varied diets containing vegetables, beans, grains, nuts, and seeds rarely have any difficulty getting enough protein as long as their diet contains enough energy (calories) to support growth. There is no need to take protein supplements. There is no health benefit to eating a very high protein diet and it will not help in muscle building.

During adolescence, calcium is used to build bones. The density of bones is determined in adolescence and young adulthood, and so it is important to include three or more good sources of calcium in a teenager's diet every day.

Cow's milk and dairy products do contain calcium. However, there are other good sources of calcium such as tofu processed with calcium sulfate, green leafy vegetables including collard greens, mustard greens, and kale, as well as tahini (sesame butter).

By eating a varied diet, a vegan can meet his or her iron needs, while avoiding the excess fat and cholesterol found in red meats such as beef or pork. To increase the amount of iron absorbed from a meal, eat a food containing vitamin C as part of the meal. Citrus fruits and juices, tomatoes, and broccoli are all good sources of vitamin C. Foods that are high in iron include broccoli, raisins, watermelon, spinach, black-eyed peas, blackstrap molasses, chickpeas, and pinto beans.

It is important to consume adequate vitamin B12 during adolescence. Vitamin B12 is not found in plants. Some cereals such as Nutri-Grain have vitamin B12 (check the label). Red Star T-6635 + nutritional yeast also supplies vitamin B12.

Many teenagers are concerned with losing or gaining weight. To lose weight, look at the diet. If it has lots of sweet or fatty foods, replace them with fruits, vegetables, grains, and legumes. If a diet already seems healthy, increased exercise -- walking, running or swimming daily -- can help control weight. To gain weight, more calories are needed. Perhaps eating more often or eating foods somewhat higher in fat and lower in bulk will help. Try to eat three or more times a day whether you are trying to gain weight or lose weight. It is hard to get all of the nutritious foods you need if you only eat one meal a day. If you feel that you cannot control your eating behavior or if you are losing a great deal of weight, you should discuss this with your health care provider.

Often there is just not enough time to eat. Here are some foods that kids can eat on the run. Some of these foods can be found in fast-food restaurants -- check the menu. Ideas for snacks that you can carry from home include:

Apples, oranges, bananas, grapes, peaches, plums, dried fruits, bagels and peanut butter, carrot or celery sticks, popcorn, pretzels, soy cheese pizza, bean tacos or burritos, salad, soy yogurt, soy milk, rice cakes, sandwiches, frozen juice bars.

References

1. Specker BL, Valanis B, Hertzberg V et al: Sunshine exposure and serum 25-hydroxyvitamin D concentrations in exclusively breast-fed infants. *J Pediatr* 107: 372-376, 1985.

2. Specker BL, Greer F, Tsang RC: Vitamin D. In Tsang RC and Nichols BL (eds): *Nutrition During Infancy.* Philadelphia: Hanley & Belfus, Inc., 1988; 264-276.

3. Hergenrather J, Hlady G, Wallace B, Savage E: Pollutants in breast milk of vegetarians. *New Engl J Med* 304: 792, 1981.

4. Purvis GA, Bartholmey SJ: Infant feeding practices: Commercially pre-pared baby foods. In Tsang RC and Nichols BL (eds): *Nutrition During Infancy.* Philadelphia: Hanley & Belfus, Inc., 1988; 399-417.

5. Robertson L, Flinders C, Ruppenthal B: *The New Laurel's Kitchen. A Handbook for Vegetarian Cookery and Nutrition.* Berkley, CA: Ten Speed Press, 1986.

6. Fulton JR, Hutton CW, Stitt KR: Preschool vegetarian children. *J Am Diet Assoc* 76: 360-365, 1980.

7. Sanders TAB and Purves R: An anthropometric and dietary assessment of the nutritional status of vegan pre-school children. *J Hum Nutr* 35: 349-357, 1981.

8. Shinwell ED and Gorodischer R: Totally vegetarian diets and infant nutrition. *Pediatrics* 70: 582-586, 1982.

9. O'Connell JM, Dibley MJ, Sierra J et al: Growth of vegetarian children: The Farm study. *Pediatrics* 84: 475-481, 1989.

10. Truesdell DD and Acosta PB: Feeding the vegan infant and child. *J Am Diet Assoc* 85: 837-840, 1985.

11. Vyhmeister IB, Register UD, Sonnenberg LM: Safe vegetarian diets for children. *Pediatr Clin N Amer* 24: 203-210, 1977.

12. Food and Nutrition Board, National Research Council: *Recommended Dietary Allowances,* 10th ed. Washington, DC: National Academy Press, 1989.

13. Satter E: *Child of Mine. Feeding with Love and Good Sense.* Palo Alto, CA: Bull Publishing Co., 1986.

Nutrition Glossary

Absorption - taking up nutrients into the blood from the stomach and small and large intestines. Nutrients must be absorbed in order to be used by the body.

Adequate - providing all of the essential nutrients, fiber, and energy in amounts which are enough to meet needs.

Amino acids - building blocks of protein. There are nine amino acids which the human body cannot make in amounts high enough to meet needs. These are called essential amino acids and must be present in one's diet.

Anemia, iron deficiency - reduction in the size of red blood cells due to iron deficiency. Smaller red blood cells are less able to carry oxygen to meet the needs of the body.

Availability - how well a nutrient can be absorbed.

Calorie - a measure of the amount of energy provided by a food. A chemist would define a calorie as the amount of heat needed to raise the temperature of a liter of water 1 degree Celsius.

Carbohydrate - a compound which is made of simple sugars or groups of simple sugars. Carbohydrates are often called sugars and starches.

Cholesterol, blood - the amount of cholesterol found in the blood. High blood cholesterol levels are associated with greater risk for heart disease. Blood cholesterol levels below 200 milligrams per 100 milliliters of blood are recommended by the American Heart Association and other public health groups to reduce the risk of developing heart disease.

Cholesterol, dietary - the amount of cholesterol which occurs in the diet. Cholesterol is a waxy substance, found only in foods of animal origin. Diets which are high in cholesterol have been associated with increased risk of heart disease. It is not necessary to have any cholesterol in the diet because the human body makes all the cholesterol it needs.

Complex carbohydrate - starches or fiber. There are 2 basic types of carbohydrates: complex and simple. Simple carbohydrates are also called sugars.

Diet - a style or way of eating.

Dietary fiber - the fiber in foods which resists human digestion.

Dietitian - often used as a short name for a registered dietitian (see definition). However, in many states the title "dietitian" is not legally protected and can be used by anyone.

Digestion - the physical and chemical breaking down of food to a form which can be used by the body.

Essential - description of a nutrient which cannot be produced by the body in amounts high enough to meet needs.

Fat - an oily or greasy material which is found in animal tissue and plant seeds. The term fat is often used to mean both fats and oils. Lipid is another term which is used for fat.

Fiber - the part of food which is not digested by humans.

Food and Nutrition Board - a section of the National Academy of Sciences which oversees the production of the Recommended Dietary Allowances.

Gram - a unit for measuring weight. A gram is the weight of 1 cubic centimeter or 1 milliliter of water under defined conditions of temperature and pressure. Commonly abbreviated gm.

HDL (high density lipoprotein) cholesterol - often called "good cholesterol". HDL cholesterol is measured as part of a blood lipid profile. Higher levels of HDL appear to reduce the risk of heart disease.

Hydrogenated fat - an unsaturated fat which has had hydrogen added to it in processing to make it more solid and more like a saturated fat. Many margarines and other processed foods contain hydrogenated fats.

LDL (low density lipoprotein) cholesterol - often called "bad cholesterol". LDL cholesterol is measured as a part of a blood lipid profile. Higher levels of LDL appear to increase the risk of heart disease. The level of LDL cholesterol can often be reduced by reducing the amount of saturated fat and cholesterol in one's diet.

Microgram - 1/1,000,000 of a gram. Commonly abbreviated mcg.

Milligram - 1/1,000 of a gram. Commonly abbreviated mg.

Mineral - a naturally occurring, inorganic substance. Some essential minerals include calcium, iron, sodium, and zinc.

Monounsaturated fat - canola, olive, and peanut oils are all high in monounsaturated fats. A monounsaturated fat has a chemical structure which includes one double bond.

National Academy of Sciences - a private non-profit group which advises the United States government on science and health issues.

Nutrient - a component of food that helps to nourish the body. Nutrients are classified as protein, fats, carbohydrates, vitamins, minerals, and water.

Nutrition - the science that interprets the relationship of food and diet to the function and health of a living being.

Nutritionist - in some states, by legal definition, refers to an individual with advanced degrees (masters or Ph.D.) in nutrition or a related field from an accredited institution. In other states, this term is not regulated and can be used by anyone.

Obesity - excessive body fatness. Obesity is most often determined by comparing body weight with tables of ideal weight for a specific height. The person whose weight is 20% or more above the table weight is termed obese.

Osteoporosis - a condition in which bones become porous and brittle.

Overweight - weight which is 10% or more above the recommended weight for a specific height.

Polyunsaturated fat - A fat which is usually liquid at room temperature. Safflower, sunflower, corn, and soybean oils are all high in polyunsaturated fat. Polyunsaturated fats have a chemical structure which includes more than one double bond.

Protein - a nutrient which contains nitrogen and is made up of amino acids.

Recommended Dietary Allowance (RDA) - the level of intake of an essential nutrient, that, on the basis of scientific knowledge, is judged by the Food and Nutrition Board of the National Academy of Sciences to be adequate to meet the known needs of practically all healthy persons.

Registered Dietitian (R.D.) - an individual who has a degree in nutrition and food sciences from an accredited institution, has completed a year or more of clinical internship or other approved experience, and has passed a national examination. R.D.'s are also required to maintain up-to-date knowledge of nutrition through continuing education.

Requirement - the amount of a nutrient which will just prevent the development of deficiency symptoms. Requirements are different from recommendations since recommendations usually are more generous.

Saturated fat - a fat which is usually solid at room temperature. Coconut and palm oils and animal fats are especially high in saturated fat. Saturated fat has a chemical structure which includes no double bonds.

U.S. RDA - the figures used for comparison on food labels wherever nutrition labels are required, also called the United States Recommended Daily Allowances. The amount of a nutrient in a food is compared to the U.S. RDA and expressed as a percentage of the U.S. RDA on the label. See Table 19 (page 203) for the current U.S. RDAs for adults.

Varied diet - a diet which includes different foods, the opposite of a monotonous diet.

Vegan - a vegetarian who does not use any animal products such as eggs, dairy products, wool, and leather.

Vegetarian - a person who chooses to abstain from meat, fish, and poultry.

Vitamin - a compound which is essential for life and is needed in very small amounts.

Table 19: U.S. RDA for Adults

Protein	65 gm
Vitamin A	5000 IU
Vitamin C	60 mg
Thiamin	1.5 mg
Riboflavin	1.7 mg
Niacin	20 mg
Calcium	1000 mg
Iron	18 mg
Vitamin D	400 IU
Vitamin E	30 IU
Vitamin B6	2 mg
Folacin	0.4 mg
Vitamin B12	6 mcg
Phosphorus	1000 mg
Iodine	150 mcg
Magnesium	400 mg
Zinc	15 mg
Copper	2 mg
Biotin	0.3 mg
Pantothenic acid	10 mg

RECOMMENDED READING LIST

Books:

Child of Mine. Feeding with Love and Good Sense. By E. Satter. Bull Publishing Company, 1986.

The New Laurel's Kitchen. A Handbook for Vegetarian Cookery and Nutrition. By L. Robertson, C. Flinders, and B. Ruppenthal., Ten Speed Press, 1986.

The Power of Your Plate. By N.D. Barnard. Book Publishing Company, 1990.

Pregnancy, Children, and the Vegan Diet. By M. Klaper. Gentle World, 1987.

Raising Your Family Naturally. By J. Gross. Lyle Stuart, Inc., 1983.

Vegetarian Journal Reports. Edited by D. Wasserman and C. Stahler. The Vegetarian Resource Group, 1990.

Vegan Nutrition. By G. Langley. The Vegan Society Ltd., 1988.

A Vegetarian Sourcebook. By K. Akers. Vegetarian Press, 1989.

Periodicals:

Nutrition Action Health Letter, Center for Science in the Public Interest, 1875 Connecticut Avenue, NW, Suite 300, Washington, D.C. 20009-5728

Nutrition Week, Community Nutrition Institute, 2001 S Street, N.W., Washington, D.C. 20009

Vegetarian Gourmet, Chitra Publications, 2 Public Avenue, Montrose, PA 18801-1220.

Vegetarian Journal, The Vegetarian Resource Group, P.O. Box 1463, Baltimore, MD 21203

Vegetarian Times, Vegetarian Times, P.O. Box 446, Mt. Morris, IL 61054-8081

CRUELTY-FREE SHOPPING BY MAIL

Note: The following pages contain the names of companies and organizations offering cruelty-free products, including vegan food, cosmetics and household products that have not been tested on animals and are environmentally sound, as well as clothes and accessories not made with animal products. In addition, this section lists places to buy educational materials on these topics and a bibliography.

Three years ago when this book was conceived, few mail-order companies sold vegan items. In the past year many cruelty-free mail-order companies have started. We hope that readers of *Simply Vegan* will support these companies and tell them that they first heard about them in this book. Please let us know if any of these companies change their address or go out of business. In addition, because this book will be updated from time to time, please send us the names and addresses of any other cruelty-free mail-order companies that are not listed here.

Please send a donation to these companies when requesting a catalog in order to help them survive!

VEGAN FOOD THROUGH THE MAIL

Condiments
Jasmine and Bread, Inc., RR #2, Box 256, South Royalton, VT 05068, offers a wide variety of condiments including *Beyond Catsup, Plum Perfect, Beyond Horseradish Mustard,* and *Serious Sauce* for barbecuing. Many of their products contain no salt and additives.

Cultures
Those who live in urban areas usually do not have trouble buying tofu or tempeh. However, for those who cannot locate soy products in their area or city dwellers who would like to try making their own tempeh and other soy products, the following companies should be of help. **The Farm Tempeh Lab**, P.O. Box 280, Summertown, TN 38483, sells Rhizosporus oligosporus culture for making tempeh commercially and at home. **Gem Cultures**, 30301 Sherwood Road, Fort Bragg, CA 95437, offers a tempeh starter, miso, amazake, shoyu, tamari starters, coagulants for curdling tofu, and a fresh sourdough culture.

Fruits and Vegetables

Organic Foods Express, 11003 Emack Road, Beltsville, MD 20708, offers fresh organic produce. Although not organic, several other companies offer fruits and vegetables in season by mail. Cases of different kinds of fruit can be ordered each month from **Harry and David**, Bear Creek Orchards, Medford, OR 97501 or call (800) 547-3033 to request a catalog. **J.R. Brooks and Son**, P.O. Drawer 9, Homestead, FL 33090 or call (305) 247-3544 offers quality tropical fruits and vegetables, including items that are often difficult to locate. **Gold Mine Natural Food Company**, 1947 30th Street, San Diego, CA 92102 or call (800) 475-FOOD offers organic foods, books, and household products.

Herbs and Spices

Old New Orleans Food and Spices, Progress Grocery Co., 915 Decatur Street, New Orleans, LA 70116; **Rosemary's Garden**, P.O. Box 1940, Redway, CA 95560; and **San Francisco Herb and Natural Food Company**, P.O. Box 40604, San Francisco, CA 94140, all offer catalogs with a list of herbs and/or spices.

Kosher Health Foods

Healthy Instincts, P.O. Box 653, Long Beach, NY 11561, is a mail-order business that offers healthy kosher certified foods, many of which are vegan.

Lightweight Foods for Backpacking and Cycling

Milford's Lightweight Foods, 315 Flat Creek Road, Black Mountain, NC 28711, offers dried food, much of which is vegan, that is great for long distance hikers and bikers.

Natural Foods Products Mail-Order Companies

The list of companies that offer natural foods products through the mail continues to skyrocket. The following is a partial list. Some companies may insist on a minimum dollar amount for your catalog, which they will apply to your first order. **Arrowhead Mills**, P.O. Box 2059, Hereford, TX 79045; **Deer Valley Farms**, RD1, Guilford, NY 13780; **Frankferd Farms**, 318 Love Road, RD 1, Valencia, PA 16059; **Garden Spot Distributors (Shiloh Farms)**, Rt. 1, Box 729 A, New Holland, PA 17557; **Lundberg Brown Rice, Wehah Farms, Inc.**, 5370 Church Street, P.O. Box 369, Richvale, CA 95974; **Maine Coast Sea Vegetables**, Franklin, ME 04634; **Maine Seaweed Company**,

Box 57, Steuben, ME 04680; **Jaffe Brothers, Inc.**, P.O. Box 636, Valley Center, CA 92082; **Mendocino Sea Vegetables Company**, P.O. Box 372, Navarro, CA 95463; **Mountain Ark Trader** (macrobiotic foods), 120 South East Avenue, Fayetteville, AR 72701; **Natural Lifestyle Supplies**, 16 Lookout Drive, Asheville, NC 28804; **Neshaminy Valley Natural Foods**, 5 Louise Drive, Ivyland, PA 18974; **Ozark Cooperative Warehouse**, 401 Watson Street, P.O. Box 30, Fayetteville, AR 72701; **Quinoa Corporation**, 2300 Central Avenue, Boulder, CO 80301; **Tree of Life Distribution**, 1750 Tree Blvd., St. Augustine, FL 32086; **Tree of Life Midwest**, 225 Daniels Way, Bloomington, IN 47404; and **Walnut Acres**, Penns Creek, Pa 17862.

Organic Food Mail-Order Suppliers
Americans for Safe Food, 1875 Connecticut Avenue NW, #300, Washington, DC 20009, provides a complete list of organic food mail-order suppliers in the United States.

Organic Seeds for Growing Organic Plants
Seeds of Change, 621 Old Santa Fe Trail, #10, Santa Fe, NM, 87501, offers organic seeds that are not hybrids.

Sprouts
The Sprout House, PO Box 1100, Great Barrington, MA 01230, sells seeds for home sprouting.

Vegan Frostings, Hot Cocoa, Dip for Strawberries, and Other Chocolate Lovers' Delights
Wax Orchards, Rt. 4-320, Vashon, WA 98070, offers the above products as well as a variety of sweet fudge toppings and a concentrated fruit juice sweetener. All items are dairy-free and contain no refined white sugar.

Vegan Soyfoods

Many soy cheeses contain casein, which is an animal product. Make sure you check labels. *Soymage*, available from **Soyco Foods**, P.O. Box 5181, Newcastle, PA 16105, is a vegan cheese. A great alternative to hotdogs is *Tofu Pups*, produced by **Lightlife Foods, Inc.**, P.O. Box 870, Greenfield, MA 01302. This company also produces a soy alternative for bologna. Another delicious soy weiner is produced by **Yves Fine Foods**, Vancouver, British Columbia, Canada. They also produce Tofu Garden Patties. Several companies make soy mayonnaise including **Nasoya Foods**, Leominster, MA 01454, which offers *Soyanaise*, and **Hain Pure Foods Co., Inc.**, which offers *Hain Eggless Mayonnaise*. An alternative sausage is available from **Spring Creek Soy Dairy**, Spencer, WV 25276. Their product is called *soysage*. Soy milk is produced by several companies today including **Ah–Soy**, Great Eastern Sun, P.O. Box 327, Enka, NC 28728; **Westbrae Natural Foods Inc.**, P.O. Box 91-1181, Commerce, CA 90091; **EdenSoy, Eden Foods, Inc.**, 701 Tecumseh Road, Clinton, MI 49236; and **Vitasoy USA Inc.**, 99 Park Lane, Brisbane, CA 94005. Soy ice cream also can be found in many supermarkets in freezer cases. As we go to press, **Archer Daniels Midland** (ADM) has introduced a vegan soy burger both in a dry mix and frozen form. Already, **Fantastic Foods**, 106 Galli Drive, Novato, CA 94947, offers several burger mixes that are quick and easy to prepare. Expect to see a sharp increase in the number of soy products available in stores throughout the 1990's.

Wild and Seasonal Salads

Pragtree Farm, 13217 Mattson Road, Arlington, WA 98223, offers organic fresh, wild salad greens, salad herbs, and edible flowers. Pragtree Farm is nestled in the foothills of Washington's Cascade Mountains. The farm is owned by the Evergreen Land Trust, a non-profit corporation established to make land available for community and environmental purposes.

VEGAN FOOD PRODUCTS

You may have trouble finding certain vegan foods in your neighborhood, especially if you do not live in a city. For this reason, we have added the following list of vegan products you may not have access to. Try to get your local supermarket or natural foods store to carry these products. If this fails, write to the companies and ask them how you can obtain these items.

Allied Old English, Inc., 100 Markley Street, Port Reading, NJ 07064 offers *Sorrel Ridge* unsweetened fruit only conserves, as well as *Hot Cha Cha Texas Salsa*; **Beatrice/Hunt-Wesson Foodservice**, 1645 W. Valencia, Fullerton, CA 92633-3899, or call (800) 633-0112, sells *Rosarita Refried Beans* containing no lard and which is available in institutional sizes, too; **Downeast Basics, Inc.**, RFD 3, Box 99, Bangor, ME 04401 sells *Simply Pure*, an organic baby food line; **Earth's Best**, PO Box 887, Middlebury, VT 05753 offers organic baby food; **East Wind Nut Butter**, East Wind Community, Inc., Box Pl, Tecumseh, MO 65760 sells natural peanut butter, tahini or sesame butter, cashew butter, and almond butter; **Ener-G Foods**, Inc., 5960 1st Avenue, PO Box 84487, Seattle, WA 98124-5787 offers a vegan egg replacer and other vegan products; **Fantastic Foods, Inc.**, 106 Galli Drive, Novato, CA 94949 sells numerous vegan food products, including instant refried beans, tabouli, falafal, tempura batter, nature burgers, chili, pilafs, and pasta salads; **Janeric Products**, Box 386, Johnson, VT 05656 produces Kosher, 100% *Vermont Maple Products*; this company does not use animal fat to keep the boiling maple syrup from foaming; **Loma Linda Foods Inc.**, 11503 Pierce Street, Riverside, CA 92515 sells *Soyagen*, which is soy powder to make soy milk; they also sell other vegetarian products, but they tend to be high in sodium; **More Than Foods, Inc.**, PO Box 1103, McLean, VA 22101 sells several pilaf mixes, as well as potato mixes, that are light and easy to carry while hiking; **Sprout Delights, Inc.**, 13090 NW 7th Avenue, Miami, FL 33168 sells Kosher vegan baked goods that are made out of sprouts; **Super Soynuts**, Lee Seed Company, Inc., RR 1, Inwood, IA 51240 sells soynut butter, a great alternative for people allergic to nut butters.

VEGAN VITAMINS

Freeda Vitamins, 36 East 41 Street, New York, NY 10017, and **Vegetarian Products Company**, 465 Production Street, San Marcos, CA 92069, offer vegan vitamins that do not contain animal gelatin. [We do not recommend taking vitamins unless highly recommended by your doctor or nutritionist.]

CRUELTY–FREE COSMETICS
VEGAN/NOT TESTED ON ANIMALS

Note: Some mail-order companies sell only strictly vegan cosmetics; that is, the product has not been tested on animals and contains no animal products. However, many mail-order companies sell cosmetics that have not been tested on animals, but may contain animal products. Most of these companies indicate which items are vegan. Below is a list of both types of companies.

All Things Wise and Wonderful, P.O. Box 267, Pierrefonds Station, Pierre-fonds, Quebec, Canada H9H 4K9; **Amberwood**, Route 1, Box 206, Milner, GA 30257; **Animals Love Us!**, 5 Hibbert Court, Pacifica, CA 94044-1916 or call (415) 355-5557; **Basically Natural**, 109 East G Street, Brunswick, MD 21716; **Beauty Without Cruelty, Ltd.**, 451 Queen Anne Road, Teaneck, NJ 07666; **The Body Shop, Inc.**, 45 Horsehill Road, Hanover Technical Center, Cedar Knolls, NJ 07927-2003 or call (800) 541-2535; **A Clear Alternative**, 8707 West Lane, Magnolia, TX 77355; **The Compassionate Consumer**, PO Box 27, Jericho, NY 11753; **Earthsafe Products**, PO Box 81061, Cleveland, OH 44181-9933; **Ecco Bella**, 6 Provost Square, Suite 602, Caldwell, NJ 07006; **Eco–Choice**, PO Box 281, Montvale, NJ 07645-0281; **Humane Alternative Products**, 8 Hutchins Street, Concord, NH 03301; **Humane Street USA**, 467 Saratoga Avenue, Suite 300, San Jose, CA 95129; **Imagine Inc.**, 1510 Squire Lane, Addison, IL 60101; **InterNatural**, PO Box 680, Shaker Street, S. Sutton, NH 03273 or call (800) 446-4903; **Kindness Products**, 7150 Morse Road, New Albany, OH 43054; **Kiss My Face Corporation**, PO Box 804, New Paltz, NY 12561; **LaCrista, Inc.**, Davidsonville, MD 21035; **Lion and Lamb, Inc.**, 29-28 41st Avenue, Suite 813, Long Island City, NY 11101; **Only Natu-ral, Inc.**, 14 Buchanan Road, Salem, MA 01970; **Orjene Natural Cosmetics**, 5-43 48th Avenue, Long Island City, NY 11101; **Rainbow Concepts**, PO Box 2332, Stone Mountain, GA 30086-2332; **Rainbow Research**, 170 Wilbur Place, Bohemia, NY 11716 or call (800) 722-9595; **Simmons Handcrafts**, 42295 Hwy 36, Bridgeville, CA 95526; **Sombra Cosmetics Inc.**, 5600-G McLeod NE, Albuquerque, NM 87109 or call (800) 225-3963; **Spare The Animals, Inc.**, PO Box 233, Tiverton, RI 02878; and **Sunrise Lane**, 780 Greenwich Street, New York, NY 10014.

In addition, write to the following groups for a complete list of cruelty-free cosmetics: **American Anti–Vivisection Society** (AAVS), Suite 204, 801 Old York Road, Jenkintown, PA 19046; **Beauty Without Cruelty** (BWC), 175 West 12th Street, New York, NY 10011; **Coalition to End Animal Suffering and Exploitation** (CEASE), Box 27, Cambridge, MA 02239; **The Humane Society of the United States** (HSUS), 2100 L Street NW, Washington, D.C. 20037; and **People for the Ethical Treatment of Animals** (PETA), Box 42516, Washington, D.C. 20014.

HOUSEHOLD PRODUCTS
VEGAN/ENVIRONMENTALLY SOUND

Atlantic Recycled Paper Company, PO Box 39096, Baltimore, MD 21212 or call (800) 323-2811; **Earth Care Paper**, Inc., PO Box 3335, Madison, WI 53704; **Earth Wise Products**, PO Box 683, Roseville, MI 48066-0683; **The Desert Sky**, 4706 N. Midkiff #30, Suite 254, Midland, TX 79705; **Good Life Products**, 39021 Byers, Sterling Heights, MI 48310; **Home Service Products Company**, PO Box 269, Bound Brook, NJ 08805; **Livos Plantchemistry** (paint), 1365 Rufina Circle, Santa Fe, NM 87501, or call (505) 438-3448; **New Age Products**, Nor'West Distributing, PO Box 1153, Port Townsend, WA 98368; **Real Goods Trading Company**, 966 Mazzoni Street, Ukiah, CA 95482, or call (800) 762-7325; **Seventh Generation**, Colchester, VT 05446-1672, or call (800) 456-1177; **Tomahawk Live Trap Company**, PO Box 323, Tomahawk, WI 54487; **Williams–Sonoma**, PO Box 7456, San Francisco, CA 94120-7456; **Wind and Water Catalogue**, 1705 14th Street, Suite 371, Boulder, CO 80302.

CLOTHING CONTAINING
NO ANIMAL PRODUCTS

Aesop Unlimited, 55 Fenno Street, PO Box 315, N. Cambridge, MA 02140 offers non-leather belts, sandals, etc.; **Deva**, Box F88, Burkittsville, MD 21718 sells all cotton clothing; **Heartland Products, Ltd.**, Box 218, Dakota City, IA 50529 sells non-leather shoes, sneakers, boots, etc.; **Lands' End, Inc.**, 1 Lands' End Lane, Dodgeville, WI 53595, or call (800) 356-4444 sells many cotton items; however, not all items are vegan; **Mother Hart's Natural Products for Home and Body**, PO Box 4229, Boynton Beach, FL 33424-4229; **Just In Case**, 2718 Main Street, Santa Monica, CA 90405 offers cruelty-free bags and gifts.

Note: **The Compassionate Shopper** published three times per year by **Beauty Without Cruelty**, 175 W 12th Street, New York, NY 10011-8275, is an excellent guide for purchasing vegan clothing. Send $15 for a year's subscription.

BOOKS/GUIDES

Humanitarian Books, 600 East Phil-Ellena Street, Philadelphia, PA 19119 offers old rare books on vegetarianism and animal rights; **True Food**, PO Box 87, Woodstock, NY 12498 offers good information on kitchen equipment; **Vegan Resources**, PO Box 2124, Orange, CA 92669 offers a cruelty-free shopping guide.

EDUCATIONAL MATERIALS

agAcess, PO Box 2008, Davis, CA 95617 offers agricultural books, including many on organic/sustainable agriculture; **Bullfrog Films, Inc.**, Oley, PA 19547 is the distributor of the film and video called "Living the Good Life" which describes Helen and Scott Nearing's experiences on homesteading and vegetarian living; **Center for Teaching Peace**, 4501 Van Ness Street NW, Washington, DC 20016 offers lectures on non-violence, vegetarianism, animal rights, environmental concerns, etc.; **Focus on Animals**, PO Box 150, Trumbull, CT 06611 offers videos on vegetarianism/animal rights; **Great American Stock**, 7566 Trade Street, San Diego, CA 92121 sells full color photos of all foods, many of which are vegan, that are great for educational purposes/displays; **New Age Journal's Yearly Guide to New Age Living**, 342 Western Avenue Brighton, MA 02135; **Organic Producers Computer Commodity Board**, Box 9547, Kansas City, MO 64133.

MISCELLANEOUS VEGAN PRODUCTS

Calliste Intercontinental, 42030 Avenida Alvarado, Unit H, Temecula, CA 92390 sells soap; **Canada's All Natural Soap, Trianco Corporation**, 14 Buchanan Road, Salem, MA 01970; **Nature's Gate Herbal Cosmetics**, 9183 Kelvin Avenue, Chadsworth, CA 91311 sells shampoos; **NatureWorks Inc.**, 5310 Derry Avenue, Agoura Hills, CA 91301 sells soap; **Sierra Soap**, Parodon, PO Box 1863-E, Pollock Pines, CA 95726 sells handmade olive oil soap; **Tom's of Maine, Inc.**, Kennebunk, ME 04043 sells toothpaste, mouthwash, and shaving cream.

BIBLIOGRAPHY

VEGAN COOKBOOKS

The Cookbook for People Who Love Animals. Introduction by Michael A. Klaper, M.D. Gentle World, Inc., 1989.

Ecological Cooking. By Joanne Stepaniak and Kathy Hecker. Book Publishing Company, 1991.

The Lighthearted Vegetarian Gourmet. By Steve Victor. Pacific Press Publishing Association, 1988.

The McDougall Health-Supporting Cookbook. By Mary McDougall. New Win Publishing, Inc., 1985.

The New Farm Vegetarian Cookbook. Edited by Louise Hagler and Dorothy R. Bates. Book Publishing Company, 1988.

No Cholesterol Passover Recipes. By Debra Wasserman and Charles Stahler. The Vegetarian Resource Group, 1986.

The Oats, Peas, Beans & Barley Cookbook. By Edyth Young Cottrell. Woodbridge Press, 1989.

Recipes from an Ecological Kitchen. By Lorna J. Sass. William Morrow and Company, Inc., 1992.

Seattle Peace-Meal Diet. By the PAWS Resource Book Committee. George Banta Company, 1986.

The Single Vegan. By Leah Leneman. Thorsons Publishing Group, 1989.

The Tempeh Cookbook. By Dorothy R. Bates. Book Publishing Company, 1989.

The Vegan Cookbook. By Alan Wakeman and Gordon Baserville. Faber and Faber, 1986.

The Vegan Kitchen. By Freya Dinshah. Ahimsa Publications.

Vegetarian Cooking for a Better World. By Muriel C. Golde. North American Vegetarian Society.

BOOKS

Animal Factories. By Jim Mason and Peter Singer. Crown Publishers, 1990.

Beyond Beef. By Jeremy Rifkin. Dutton, 1992.

Compassion - The Ultimate Ethic. By Victoria Moran. Thorsons Publishers Limited, 1985.

Diet for a New America. By John Robbins. Stillpoint Publishing, 1987.

Old MacDonald's Factory Farm, By C. David Coats. The Continuum Publishing Company, 1989.

Pulling The Wool. By Christine Townsend. Hale & Iremonger Pty Limited, 1985.

A Vegetarian Sourcebook. By Keith Akers. Vegetarian Press, 1989.

VEGAN–ORIENTED/VEGETARIAN GROUPS

Write to *The Vegetarian Resource Group*, PO Box 1463, Baltimore, MD 21203 for information on groups in your area. Please indicate which zip codes are in your vicinity.

INDEX

INDEX OF TABLES

JOIN THE VEGETARIAN RESOURCE GROUP
RECEIVE VEGETARIAN JOURNAL

The Vegetarian Resource Group is a non-profit organization educating the public about the various aspects of vegetarianism, which is the abstinence of meat, fish, and fowl. The group publishes *Vegetarian Journal*, a bi-monthly 36-page publication, as well as other books, brochures, posters, etc. *The Vegetarian Resource Group* also sponsors conferences and events for the public.

* MEMBERSHIP APPLICATION *

NAME _____

ADDRESS _____

_____ ZIP _____

TELEPHONE _____

Send $20.00 check to *The Vegetarian Resource Group*, PO Box 1463, Baltimore, MD 21203. Call (410) 366-VEGE with questions. Members receive *Vegetarian Journal*.

OTHER BOOKS PUBLISHED BY
THE VEGETARIAN RESOURCE GROUP

MEATLESS MEALS FOR WORKING PEOPLE -- QUICK AND EASY VEGETARIAN RECIPES: Most of the recipes are vegan, but not all. Cost: $6.00

NO CHOLESTEROL PASSOVER RECIPES: All recipes are vegan. Includes ideas for a vegetarian seder. Cost: $5.00

I LOVE ANIMALS AND BROCCOLI: A children's activity book for kids that can read. Covers topics such as health, ecology, world hunger, and animal rights. Cost: $5.00

VEGETARIAN JOURNAL REPORTS: Features a 28 day meal plan, weight loss guide, information for athletes, egg replacers, sugar substitutes, dairy substitutes, hospital survival guide, Indian vegetarian recipes, diabetes and a vegetarian diet, non-leather shoe information, plus many other articles and recipes (most are vegan). Cost: $10.00

ALSO AVAILABLE FROM THE VEGETARIAN RESOURCE GROUP

VEGAN QUANTITY RECIPE PACKET: Includes 28 vegan recipes (entrees, side dishes, soups, etc.) with serving sizes of 25 and 50, as well as a list of suppliers of vegetarian food available in institutional sizes. Cost: $15.00

BROCHURES FOR TABLING: General vegetarian information, teenagers and the vegetarian diet, animal rights, living your ethics/career choices, etc.

EDUCATIONAL MATERIALS FOR CLASSROOMS: Lesson plans, coloring book, handouts for older children, etc.

ADDITIONAL COPIES OF SIMPLY VEGAN: $12 per book. Inquire about quantity discounts for stores and non-profit groups.

**Write or send check to The Vegetarian Resource Group,
PO Box 1463, Baltimore, MD 21203 or call (410) 366–VEGE.**